Meditations on Mary

Other books by Jacques-Bénigne Bossuet
from Sophia Institute Press:

Meditations for Advent
Meditations for Lent

Jacques-Bénigne Bossuet

Meditations on Mary

Edited and translated
by Christopher O. Blum

SOPHIA INSTITUTE PRESS
Manchester, New Hampshire

Copyright 2015 by Christopher O. Blum

Meditations on Mary is a selection and translation of the Scriptural meditations and sermons of Jacques-Bénigne Bossuet (1627–1704), as found in these editions of the French: *Élévations à Dieu sur tous les mystères de la religion chrétienne*, in *Oeuvres complètes de Bossuet*, edited by Abbé Guillaume (Lyon: Briday, 1879), and *Oeuvres Oratoires de Bossuet*, édition critique de l'abbé J. Lebarq, revue et augmentée par Ch. Urbain et E. Levesque, 7 volumes (Paris: Desclée de Brouwer, 1914–1926).

Printed in the United States of America. All rights reserved.

Cover design by Perceptions Design Studio.

Unless otherwise noted, biblical references are taken from the Catholic Edition of the Revised Standard Version of the Bible, copyright 1965, 1966 by the Division of Christian Education of the National Council of the Churches of Christ in the United States of America. Used by permission. All rights reserved.

No part of this book may be reproduced, stored in a retrieval system, or transmitted in any form, or by any means, electronic, mechanical, photocopying, or otherwise, without the prior written permission of the publisher, except by a reviewer, who may quote brief passages in a review.

Sophia Institute Press
Box 5284, Manchester, NH 03108
1-800-888-9344

www.SophiaInstitute.com

Sophia Institute Press® is a registered trademark of Sophia Institute.

Library of Congress Cataloging-in-Publication Data
Bossuet, Jacques Bénigne, 1627-1704.
  [Works. Selections. English. 2015]
  Meditations on Mary / Jacques-Benigne Bossuet ; edited and translated by Christopher O. Blum.
     pages cm
  ISBN 978-1-62282-307-9 (pbk. : alk. paper)
  1. Mary, Blessed Virgin, Saint—Meditations. 2. Mary, Blessed Virgin, Saint—Biography. I. Blum, Christopher Olaf, 1969- translator. II. Title.
  BT603.B6713 2015
  232.91—dc23
                                                         2015026390

First printing

Contents

1. The True Eve 3
2. Dispensed from the Law of Death 7
3. Set Apart 12
4. Preserved by Love 17
5. He Chose Mary for Himself 23
6. United in Spirit 30
7. The Humility of God 35
8. The Gospel Embraces the Law 41
9. Gratitude for Grace 46
10. The Magnificat 51
11. Bethlehem 59
12. Wonder 64

13. The Flight to Egypt 68

14. The Holy Family 72

15. In Her Heart 78

16. Pierced by a Sword 82

17. At the Cross 89

18. Behold Thy Mother 96

19. New Life 102

20. God Alone 107

21. A Happy Death 112

22. Glorified by Purity 117

23. Crowned with Humility 122

24. Jesus through Mary 126

Meditations on Mary

1

The True Eve

We marvel as we read the extraordinary words used by the Fathers of the Church when speaking of the most holy Virgin. From St. Irenaeus: "Condemned to death by a virgin, the human race was saved by a Virgin." Tertullian: "What was led astray into perdition by this sex was restored to salvation by this sex." And the incomparable Augustine: "By a woman, death; by a woman, life. By Eve, ruin; by Mary, salvation."

We must not think that such faithful servants of Jesus Christ wanted to lessen the honor due to their Master by associating Mary with him in this way. Truly, we misunderstand God if we think that his glory would be diminished by being shared with his creatures. God is not like us: in giving away a part, he retains the whole. If this seems strange, consider that God is the only one who can give without loss. He does not act as we do, for we divide our cares among many so that the burden on each may be less. It is not so with the living God. When he joins his creatures to his work, it is not to unburden himself, but to honor them, and so all of the glory remains his. When the Fathers taught us that Mary was associated in a singular way with the great work of the Son of God, they in no way diminished the Savior's glory.

To understand why it was fitting for the Blessed Virgin to have had such a role in the work of our salvation, we must look back to the origin of all things. There we see just how considerate God is: in the work of regenerating our nature, he employed all that had once contributed to its ruin. It is certain that God could have delivered mankind without becoming a man. Yet it pleased him to redeem us by becoming a man so that the same nature that had been enslaved by the demon could win the victory over him and his overbold companions. Even when the Son of God had resolved to come to earth and to clothe himself in human flesh, he could have made himself a body and a soul without the assistance of his creatures and thus been spared the shame of belonging to a criminal line. Nevertheless, his incomprehensible providence disposed otherwise. It pleased him that grace and blessing should find its origin in this accursed race. Our Lord wanted to be the son of Adam so that his blessed birth would forever sanctify the race that had been infected by sin.

The True Eve

Since both man and woman participated in the despoiling of our nature, they would also participate in its restoration. If the corruption of sin had dishonored both sexes, it was necessary that the Redeemer of man should honor them both. That is why, as St. Augustine tells us, Jesus Christ, a man, was born of a woman. And because mankind was cast into eternal damnation by a man and a woman, it was fitting that God should have predestined a new Eve as well as a new Adam, so as to replace the old line that had been condemned with a new line sanctified by grace. We may, therefore, conclude that just as the first Eve was the mother of all those condemned to die, so the new Eve, Mary, is the mother of all the living—that is, the faithful.

Let us compare Eve and Mary. The work of our corruption began with Eve; the work of our regeneration began with Mary. An angel of darkness spoke to Eve; an angel of light spoke to Mary. The angel of darkness wished to raise Eve to the false dignity of pretending to be divine, saying to her, "You will be like God" (Gen. 3:5). The angel of light identified Mary's true dignity as her friendship with God, saying, "The Lord is with you" (Luke 1:28). The angel of darkness, speaking to Eve, sought to incite her to rebellion: "Did God say, 'You shall not eat of any tree of the garden'?" (Gen. 3:1). The angel of light, speaking to Mary, persuaded her to be obedient: "Do not be afraid, Mary.... [W]ith God, nothing will be impossible" (Luke 1:30, 37). The word of death was spoken to Eve, the word of life to the Blessed Virgin. Eve believed the serpent, Mary the angel. Thus, as Tertullian said, "A pious faith erased the fault of an audacious credulity, and Mary repaired by her belief in God what Eve had ruined by believing the devil." Eve, led astray by the demon, was forced to flee the presence of God, whereas Mary, instructed by the angel, was made worthy to bear God, so that, as the holy martyr Irenaeus said, "The Virgin Mary became the advocate for the virgin Eve."

It cannot be doubted that Mary was the Eve of the new covenant and consequently the Mother of a new people. And Mary will be your Mother, if you live in our Lord Jesus Christ. She will be Eve—that is, in the Hebrew tongue, the living one. Adam gave this name to his wife because she was the mother of all the living. Yet it is not Eve who is the mother of all the living; she is, rather, the mother of those who will die. In fact, the first Eve received her name as a prefiguration of the Blessed Virgin, whose dignity she represents. The Blessed Virgin is the true Eve, the true Mother of all the living. Live, then, and Mary will be your Mother. But live in and through Jesus, because Mary herself has no life except in and through Jesus.

2

Dispensed from the Law of Death

A universal law of death has been declared. Would its authority be undermined if a dispensation from it were to be made? St. Paul assures us that "one man's trespass led to condemnation for all" (Rom. 5:18). He had in view the authority of the law, which in itself extends universally, but he did not deny the sovereign's power to grant dispensations. By virtue of the law's authority, Mary was condemned with the rest of the human race. Yet by the sovereign's grace and power, a dispensation was made in her favor.

A dispensation must have three characteristics if the sacred majesty of the law is to be preserved: its recipient must be eminently worthy, it must be founded on precedent, and it must enhance the sovereign's glory. Should all three of these features be found together, it would be reasonable to expect a dispensation. Let us consider them in the case of the Blessed Virgin.

Meditations on Mary

We fear that dispensations will undermine the rule of law. Yet in this case, is there anything to fear? There is only cause for fear if other cases are similar. Is there another Mother of God? Is there another Virgin and Mother to whom we ought to extend Mary's privileges? Who does not realize that this glorious maternity, this eternal alliance contracted with God, places her in a rank all her own, one that allows no comparison? With such inequality, can there be anything to fear from a dispensation?

Then there is the question of precedent. We learn from history that once the graces of a sovereign begin to follow a certain course, they flow profusely. Beneficence leads to further beneficence. God himself tells us in his Gospel: "to every one who has more will be given" (Matt. 25:29). He loves to give to those who have; he is so generous that one grace is always the pledge of many more.

This much do we see in the case of the Blessed Virgin. If we were to think her subject to the common order, we would perhaps suspect that she was conceived in sin like all other men. If, however, we recognize an almost universal dispensation from the common order; if we see her as the Catholic Faith sees her; if we see that she gives birth without agony and that her body does not decay and her senses do not rebel; if her spouse was only her guardian, her marriage a sacred veil to cover and to

Dispensed from the Law of Death

protect her virginity, and her beloved Son a flower born of her integrity; if, when she conceived him, an astonished and bewildered nature believed all its laws to have been forever abolished; if, in a word, everything is singular in Mary, then who could believe that there was nothing supernatural in the conception of so privileged a creature or that the first moment of her life would have been the only one untouched by grace?

In the third place, the glory of the sovereign—Jesus Christ himself—is plainly engaged. Princes gain what they give away when their generosity wins them honor. If Jesus honors his Mother, he brings honor to himself.

O Divine Savior, because you took on human flesh to abolish the deadly law of sin, it accords with your greatness to have abolished it in every place it once ruled. It reigned in grown men and women: Jesus destroyed it by his grace. Newborn infants groaned under its tyranny: Jesus removed it by baptism. It entered into the womb and brought death to all it found there: the Savior chose illustrious souls such as St. John the Baptist, whom he set free by sanctifying them before their birth. This law pursued us to our very origin, condemning men at the moment of their conception. O Jesus, all-powerful conqueror, could this be the one place your conquest fails to reach? Your blood, that divine remedy with so much power to deliver us from evil, has it no power to prevent evil? Is it able only to cure? Can it not preserve? And if it should be able to preserve from evil, would not this power be in vain unless there were one of your members to feel its effects? My Savior, for the sake of your glory, choose at least one creature in which all that your blood can achieve against this law will be seen! And who should this creature be, if not Mary ever-blessed?

My Savior, some will doubt the power of your blood. Yet it is most fitting that the precious blood of the Son of the Virgin should exercise all its power upon her in order to honor the place from which it came. A holy bishop once said that Mary was like all men in that she was redeemed by the blood of her Son, but unique in that this blood was brought forth from her own body. She has this in common with all the faithful: that Jesus gives her his blood; she has this all her own: that he first received it from her. She has this in common with us: that this blood was poured out upon her for her sanctification; but she has this as her own: that she was its source. We can even say that Mary's conception was the origin of the blood of Jesus. It is from this source that the stream began to flow, the stream of graces that flows in our veins by the sacraments and that brings the spirit of life to the whole body of the Church. As fountains lift their bubbling waters

Dispensed from the Law of Death

to the same height from which they have fallen, so the blood of our Savior will cause its power to be lifted up even to the conception of his Mother to honor the place from which it first flowed.

3

Set Apart

Theology teaches us that the differences we see in things are a result of Divine Wisdom. As Wisdom establishes order in things, it must also bring about the differences without which there can be no order. We see that this was the way of things from the very beginning, when, poured out upon a matter only half formed, Wisdom separated light from darkness, divided the waters below from the waters above, and sorted out the confusion of the elements.

What was done once in the Creation, Wisdom does every day in the regeneration of our nature. The material parts of the world were once separated out from what had been "without form" (Gen. 1:2); now a similar separation is made within mankind, which is one great mass of guilt. Grace saves us by a blessed separation that sets us apart from the spoiled mass, and that is the work of Wisdom, because it is Wisdom who chose us from eternity and who prepares the means by which we are justified.

Set Apart

Thus was the Blessed Virgin set apart, and this she has in common with all the faithful. To see what is extraordinary about her, we must consider her alliance with Jesus. This mystery may be appreciated with the help of the words of a venerable sermon on the Nativity: "How happy you are, peerless Mother, because you were the first to receive what was promised to all the faithful, and you alone possess the common joy of the universe." What do these words mean? If Jesus Christ is a common good, if his mysteries belong to the whole world, in what way could the Blessed Virgin possess them all alone? His death is the public sacrifice, his blood the price for all sins, his preaching the instruction for all people. And what clearly shows that he is the common good of the whole earth is that this divine Child was no sooner born than the Jews were called to him by the angels and the Gentiles by the stars.

Amid this universal liberality, Mary has a private right to possess him all alone, because she possessed him as a son. No other creature can share in this title. Only God and Mary can have the Savior for a son, and by this holy alliance Jesus gives himself to her in such a way that it may be said that the common treasure of the human race became her private property.

Thus, the Blessed Virgin was set apart, and in her separation she possesses something in common with all men and something all her own. To understand this, we must realize that we have been set apart from the rest of men and women because we belong to Jesus and have an alliance with him. But Jesus made two alliances with the Blessed Virgin: one as Savior and another as Son. The alliance with Jesus as Savior means that she must be set apart like the other faithful; the special alliance with Jesus as her Son means that she must be set apart in an extraordinary fashion.

Divine Wisdom, in the beginning you separated the elements out of the original confusion; here too there is confusion to dispel. Here is the whole of guilty mankind from which one creature must be set apart so that she may become the mother of her Creator. If the other faithful are delivered from evil, she must be preserved from it. And how? By a special communication of the privileges of her Son. He is exempt from sin, and Mary must also be exempt. O Wisdom, you have set her apart from the other faithful, but do not mix her together with her Son, because she must be infinitely beneath him. How shall we distinguish her from him, if they are both exempt from sin? Jesus was by nature, and Mary by grace; Jesus by right, and Mary by privilege and indulgence. See her thus set apart: "he who is mighty has done great things for me" (Luke 1:49).

Set Apart

Although we are not set apart in as eminent a way as the Blessed Virgin, we must not fail to be in some way. For who are the faithful people? They are a people set apart from the others, drawn forth from the mass of perdition and the universal contagion. They are a people living in the world, but not of the world. They have their treasure stored up in heaven, their home and patrimony. God has marked the foreheads of the faithful with the sacred character of baptism so that they may be set apart for him alone. Yes, Christian, if you have bound yourself to the love of this world, if you do not live as one set apart, you will lose the grace of Christ.

How shall you set yourself apart? We live in the world and are surrounded by its distractions. Must we banish ourselves from society? Must we exclude ourselves from all worldly affairs? No, but what we must do is set our hearts apart. It is by the heart that we are Christians: "man believes with his heart" (Rom. 10:10). It is the heart that must be set apart. Yet this is the chief difficulty, for it is the heart that is beset on all sides. The world flatters it and beckons to it. On one side are honors, on the other pleasures. Someone offers love; another demands it of us. How shall the heart defend itself? The task is arduous: to be always in the world but to keep one's heart set apart from its attractions. Is there any other gospel for us to follow?

Meditations on Mary

From the many useless hours that you devote to the affairs of this earth, set aside at least a few so that you may retire into yourself. Make some place of solitude for yourself, where you can meditate in secret on the sweetness of eternal goods and on the vanity of mortal things. Set yourself apart with Jesus; pour out your soul before him. Beseech him to give you the grace that will allow the attractions of heaven to draw you forth from those of this world, the grace that set apart the most holy Virgin.

4

Preserved by Love

If we see that the Son of God took on all our weaknesses, save only sin, and if his design in becoming man entailed that he did not refuse hunger, thirst, fear, sadness, or any of our other infirmities, no matter how unworthy of his greatness, then we ought to believe that he was deeply moved by filial piety, that just and holy love for those who give us life, a love impressed by nature upon our hearts. The truth is clear: it was this love that preserved the most holy Virgin in her blessed conception.

To understand this doctrine, we must note that the Blessed Virgin had a quality that distinguishes her from every other mother: she gave birth to the Giver of grace. Her Son, in this way different from every other child, was capable of acting with power from the first moment of his life. What is even more extraordinary is that the Blessed Virgin was the mother of a son who was before her. From this quality follow three beautiful effects. As Mary's Son is the dispenser of grace, he gave it to her abundantly. As he was capable of acting from the first moment of his life, he did not delay his generosity toward her, but showed it immediately. Finally, from having a Son who was before her comes this miracle: her Son's love was able to preserve her from the time of her own conception, to make her innocent. Let us ponder the love of the Son of God for the Blessed Virgin.

Have you ever wondered about the way God speaks in Sacred Scripture, how he pretends, as it were, to act as a man, by imitating our actions, our habits, and even our emotions? Sometimes he says, by the mouth of his prophets, that he has a heart made tender by compassion, sometimes that he is burning with anger, that he is appeased, that he repents, or that he has joy or sadness. What kind of mystery is this? Should God act or suffer in such ways? If the incarnate Word speaks to us in this way, we are not surprised, because he was a man. But that God, prior to being man, should speak and act as men do: this astonishes us.

You will say that God speaks in this way so as to accommodate himself to our understanding. Yes, but the Fathers teach us that God, having resolved to unite himself to our nature, did not judge it unworthy of himself to take on our sentiments beforehand. On the contrary, he

Preserved by Love

made them his own and purposefully conformed himself to them.

Can we explain so great a mystery by means of some familiar example? A man wishes to gain a high office. He prepares for it by taking on all the feelings proper to it and begins accustoming himself to the gravity of a judge or to the bravery of a soldier. God resolved to become man. He had not yet done so at the time of the prophets but had decided that he should be, and so we should not be surprised that he speaks and acts as a man before he was one, if, in some sense, it pleased him to appear to the prophets and the patriarchs with a human likeness. Why? Tertullian explained it well. These were so many preparations for the Incarnation. The one who would lower himself to the point of taking on our nature fulfilled a sort of apprenticeship by conforming himself to our sentiments. "Little by little he made himself ready to become man, and it pleased him to be from the beginning of the world what he would become in the fullness of time."

We should not, therefore, think that he waited until the day of his coming to have a son's love for the Blessed Virgin. It was enough that he had resolved to become man for him to take on every human sentiment. And if he took on human sentiments, could he have omitted those of a son, of all sentiments the most natural and most human?

Meditations on Mary

He has, therefore, always loved Mary as a mother, and he considered her as such from the very moment of her conception. Given this, could he have looked upon her in anger? Would sin belong together with so much grace, vengeance with love, enmity with friendship? Cannot Mary say with the psalmist, "[B]y my God I can leap over a wall" (Ps. 18:29)? Sin places a wall of separation, an unfriendliness, between God and man. But she says, "I can leap over the wall." How? In the name of my God, of this God who loved me as mother from the first instant of my life, of this God whose all-powerful love preserved me from the anger that menaces all the children of Eve. This is what was accomplished in the Blessed Virgin.

It is the very foundation of Christianity to understand that we did not first love God, but that he first loved us (cf. 1 John 4:10), and not only before we loved him, but while we were his enemies. The blood of the New Testament, poured out for the remission of our sins, bears witness to this truth. For if we had not been God's enemies, we would not have needed a mediator to reconcile us with him, nor a victim to appease his anger, nor blood to satisfy his justice. It is he who first loved us, by giving up his only Son for the love of us.

And you, children of God, you who love your Father: did you love him first? Or do you not confess with

Preserved by Love

the apostle that "God's love has been poured into our hearts through the Holy Spirit who has been given to us" (Rom. 5:5)? Would God have given you such a great gift if, before giving it, he had not already loved you? He has preserved us: do not doubt it. He always takes the first step. Yet he does so in order that we may approach him.

Listen to the exhortation of the psalmist: "Let us come into his presence with thanksgiving" (Ps. 95:2). This thanksgiving, however, should be joined to penance. For how can we give thanks for God's greatness any better than by humbling ourselves for our sins and falling down before his face?

Let us then fall down before him now, Christians, so that we do not fall down on that terrible day. Let us anticipate his just anger by the confession of our crimes. Let us plumb the very depths of our conscience where our enemies lie hidden. Let us descend, with a flaming torch in one hand and a sword in the other: the torch, to discover our sins by a serious examination, and the sword to cut them out at their roots by our deep sorrow. In this way, we will go before the anger of our great God, whose mercy goes always before us.

O Mary, miraculously preserved, singularly set apart, mercifully anticipated, bring aid to us in our weakness by your prayers, and obtain for us this grace, that our penance may go before the vengeance that pursues us so that we may at last be received into the kingdom of eternal peace with Father, Son, and Holy Spirit. Amen.

5

He Chose Mary for Himself

There is nothing more touching in the Gospel than the way God treats his reconciled enemies—that is, converted sinners. He is not content to wipe away the stain of their sins. It is easy for his infinite goodness to prevent our sins from hurting us; he also wants them to profit us. He bring forth so much good from them that we are constrained to bless our faults and to cry out with the Church, "O happy fault! *O felix culpa!*"[1] His graces struggle against our sins for the mastery, and it pleases him, as St. Paul said, that his "grace abound" in excess of our malice (cf. Rom. 5:20).

Moreover, he receives reconciled sinners with so much love that the most perfect innocence would seem to have grounds for complaint, or at least for jealousy. One of his sheep wanders off, and all those who remain

---

[1] From the Exultet sung at the Easter vigil.

seem much less dear to him than the one gone astray; his mercy is more tender toward the prodigal son than toward the elder brother who had always been faithful.

If this is the case, then should we say that repentant sinners are more worthy than those who have not sinned, or justice reestablished is preferable to innocence preserved? No, we must not doubt that innocence is always best.

Although we appreciate health more when it is newly restored, we do not fail to value a strong constitution over the benefit of returning health. And although it is true that our hearts are moved by the unlooked-for gift of a fine day in winter, we do not fail to prefer the constant clemency of a milder season. So, if we may regard the Savior's sentiments through a human lens, he may more tenderly caress newly converted sinners—his new conquests—but he loves the just with greater ardor, for they are his old friends.

Jesus Christ, the Son of God, is holiness itself, and although he is pleased to see at his feet the sinner who has returned to the path of righteousness, he nevertheless loves with a stronger love the innocent one who has never strayed. The innocent one approaches nearer to him and imitates him more perfectly, and so he honors him with a closer familiarity. However much beauty his

He Chose Mary for Himself

eyes may see in the tears of a penitent, it can never equal the chaste attraction of an ever-faithful holiness. These are the sentiments of Jesus according to his divine nature, but he took on other ones for the love of us when he became our Savior. God prefers the innocent, but, let us rejoice: the merciful Savior came to seek out the guilty. He lives only for sinners, because it is to sinners that he was sent.

Listen to how he explains his mission: "I came not to call the righteous" (Matt. 9:13), because, even though they may be the most worthy of my affection, my commission does not extend to them. As Savior, I must seek those who are lost; as Physician, those who are ill; as Redeemer, those who are captives. In this, he is like a physician: as a man, he is more pleased to live among the healthy, but as a physician he prefers to care for the sick. And so this good Doctor, as Son of God prefers the innocent, but as Savior seeks out the guilty. Here is the mystery illuminated by a holy and evangelical doctrine. It is full of consolation for sinners such as we are, but it also honors the holy and perpetual innocence of Mary.

For if it is true that the Son of God loves innocence so well, could it be that he would find none at all upon the earth? Shall he not have the satisfaction of seeing someone like unto himself, or who at least approaches his purity from afar? Must Jesus, the Innocent One, be always among sinners, without ever having the consolation of meeting an unstained soul? And who would that be, if not his holy Mother? Yes, let this merciful Savior, who has taken upon himself all of our guilt, spend his life running after sinners; let him go and seek them in every corner of Palestine; but let him find in his own home and under his own roof what will satisfy his eyes with the steady and lasting beauty of incorruptible holiness!

It is true that this charitable Savior does not cast off sinners, and far from sending them away from his presence, he does not disdain to call them the most honored members of his kingdom. He set the leadership of his flock in the hands of Peter, who denied him; he placed at the head of his Evangelists Matthew, who was a tax collector; he made the first of his preachers Paul, who had persecuted him. These are not innocent men; these are converted sinners whom he raised to the highest ranks. Yet you should not therefore believe that he would choose his holy Mother from the same lot. There must be a great difference between her and the others. What will that difference be?

He chose Peter, Matthew, and Paul for us, but he chose Mary for himself. For us: "whether Paul or Apollos or Cephas ... all are yours" (cf. 1 Cor. 3:22); for himself: "My

He Chose Mary for Himself

beloved is mine," and I am hers (cf. Song of Sol. 2:16). Those whom he called for others, he drew forth from sin, so that they might the better proclaim his mercy. His plan was to give hope to those souls beaten down by sin. Who could more effectively preach divine mercy than those who were themselves its illustrious examples? Who else could have said with greater effect, "The saying is sure and worthy of full acceptance, that Christ Jesus came into the world to save sinners," than a St. Paul, who was able to add, "[a]nd I am the foremost of sinners" (1 Tim. 1:15)?

Yet if he treated in this way those whom he called for the sake of us sinners, we must not think that he did the same for the dear creature, the extraordinary creature, the unique and privileged creature whom he made for himself, whom he chose to be his Mother. In his apostles and ministers, he brought about what would be most useful for the salvation of all, but in his holy Mother, he did what was sweetest, most glorious, and most satisfying for himself, and, consequently, he made Mary to be innocent. "My beloved is mine," and I am hers. The gift of innocence could not be distributed with prodigality among fallen men, but it is no excess for him to give it to his Mother, and it would have been ungenerous to have withheld it.

Meditations on Mary

No, my Savior will not do that. We see already shining forth from the newborn Mary the innocence of Jesus Christ, as a crown upon her head. Let us honor this new ray that her Son has caused to break forth upon her. "[T]he night is far gone, the day is at hand" (Rom. 13:12). Jesus will soon bring about that day by his blessed presence. O happy day, O cloudless day, O day that the innocence of the divine Jesus will make so serene and pure: when will you come to light up the world? He comes; let us rejoice. You already see the dawn breaking in the birth of the holy Virgin. Let us run with joy to see the first light of this new day. We will see shining the sweet light of an unstained purity.

We must not persuade ourselves that to distinguish Mary from Jesus we must take away her innocence and leave it to her Son alone. To tell the morning from midday, there is no need to fill the air with storms or cover the sky with clouds: it suffices that the rays of the morning sun should be weaker and their light less brilliant. To distinguish Mary from Jesus, there is no need to put sin into the mix. It suffices that her innocence be a weaker light. That light belongs to Jesus by right, but to Mary by privilege; to Jesus by nature, to Mary by grace and favor. We honor the source in Jesus, and in Mary a flowing forth from the source. What should console us is that

He Chose Mary for Himself

this flowing forth of innocence shines for the benefit of us poor sinners. Innocence normally reproaches the guilty for their evil lives and seems to pronounce condemnation upon them. Yet it is not so with Mary. Her innocence is favorable to us. And why? Because it is only a flowing forth of the innocence of the Savior Jesus. The innocence of Jesus is the life and salvation of sinners, and so the innocence of the Blessed Virgin serves to obtain pardon for sinners. Let us look upon this holy and innocent creature as the sure support for our misery and go and wash our sins in the bright light of her incorruptible purity.

6

United in Spirit

The Blessed Virgin's graces flow from her close union with Jesus Christ, and if we are to understand the effects of this union, we must take note of an important truth that is at the foundation of the gospel: the source of every grace that has adorned human nature is our alliance with Jesus Christ. This alliance opened a sacred exchange between heaven and earth that has enriched mankind immeasurably; this is why the Church, by divine inspiration, calls the Incarnation a kind of commercial exchange—O *admirabile commercium*. For, as St. Augustine said, is it not a marvelous exchange by which Jesus, the generous merchant, having come into the world like a trader to a foreign nation, sought all the wretched fruit produced by its ungrateful soil—weakness, suffering, and death—and in return brought us the true goods made in the heavenly fatherland—innocence, peace, and life everlasting? It is by this alliance that we are made wealthy;

United in Spirit

it is this marvelous exchange that gives us such a profusion of good things. This is why St. Paul assured us that we can no longer be poor, now that Jesus Christ belongs to us: "He who did not spare his own Son but gave him up for us all, will he not also give us all things with him?" (Rom. 8:32). And now that he has opened his heart to us by this boundless generosity, will not his other gifts flow freely through the same door?

If our alliance with Jesus Christ has procured such great wealth for us, then our intellect should be silent and make no attempt to explain the prerogatives of the Blessed Virgin. For if it is an incomprehensible advantage that we be given Jesus as our Savior, what shall we think of Mary, to whom the eternal Father gave him, not in the common way, but as he belongs to himself, as Son, and as only Son, as Son who, having no earthly father, received everything from his holy Mother. Does any alliance equal this one?

We must not think that this alliance united Mary to the Savior by a bodily union alone. We might at first think in these terms, but not if we consider the difference between Mary and ordinary mothers. For she is different in this: she conceived her Son in her spirit before conceiving him in her body. It is the constant teaching of the holy Fathers. How did this come about?

Meditations on Mary

It was not nature that formed the divine Child in her. She conceived him by faith; she conceived him by obedience. This is why St. Elizabeth humbly greeted Mary as the Mother of her Lord. "And why is this granted me, that the mother of my Lord should come to me?" she cried out at once, in transport. "Blessed is she who believed" (Luke 1:43, 45). It is as though she were saying: "It is true that you are a mother, but it is your faith that has made you so." Whence the holy Fathers concluded, and with one accord, that she conceived her Son in her spirit before bearing him in her body.

Do not therefore judge the Blessed Virgin as you do ordinary mothers. They do, of course, unite themselves to their children in spirit. Who could deny it? Who can fail to see them carry their children in the depth of their souls? Yet this union begins with the body and is first nourished by blood, whereas in the Blessed Virgin, the first imprint was made in her heart. Her alliance with her Son began in her spirit because she conceived him by faith.

Our Lord Jesus never unites himself to us by his body without intending to unite himself more closely in spirit. The Mystical Table, the Feast worthy of all worship, the Holy and Sacred Altar: these are the witnesses to this truth, just as are all those who approach this divine table.

United in Spirit

When you have seen Jesus Christ come to you in his own Body and Blood, when you have placed him in your mouth, do you think that he has come only to remain in your body? Please God, you know that he runs after you in search of your soul. Those who are not joined in spirit to the one whose adorable Flesh they receive have frustrated his plan and offended his love.

This is why St. Cyprian said those beautiful and terrible words: "They do violence to the Body and Blood of the Lord." Holy souls, pious souls, you who know how to taste Jesus Christ in this adorable mystery: you understand this violence. Jesus seeks the heart, and yet there are those who have stopped at the body and would remain there; they have prevented the heavenly Spouse from bringing to completion in the spirit the chaste union he seeks. They have forced him to restrain the impetuous course of the graces with which he would flood the soul. And thus his love suffers violence, and we must not be surprised if he turns in indignation and anger, and, in place of the salvation that he would bring to them, he effects their condemnation. When he unites himself bodily to us, he desires the union of spirits to be proportionate to that of the bodies.

If this be true, O holy Virgin, we understand something great about you. For such was your union to the

Meditations on Mary

body of Jesus when you conceived him in your womb that a closer one cannot be imagined. And if there had not also been a union of your spirits, his love would have been frustrated, and he would have suffered injury within you. In order to satisfy him, then, you had to be united to him in spirit as closely as you touched him by the bonds of nature and blood. And as this union was accomplished by grace, our way of thinking about you must be elevated beyond compare. Even if we should gather every gift that a creature can receive, how could all of them together hope to equal what you received?

Let us run with joy then to honor in the newborn Mary this fullness of grace. We must draw no limits to the love of the Son of God for his holy Mother.

7

The Humility of God

It is a surprising but undoubted truth that among the infinite means God has at his disposal to establish his glory, the most effective is necessarily joined to humility. He can overturn the whole of nature, he can show his power through thousands of miracles, but, by a marvelous secret, he can never cause his glory to be greater than when he abases and humiliates himself.

This we see in the mystery of the Annunciation. God wrought this great and glorious miracle when "Christ Jesus," as St. Paul said, "emptied himself, taking the form of a servant" (Phil. 2:5, 7).

God has done something new here, but what? He wished to raise his glory to its summit, and to do so, he lowered himself. He willed to reveal his glory to us at its most brilliant, and so he clothed himself in our weakness: "the Word became flesh and dwelt among us, [and] we have beheld his glory" (John 1:14). We do not meditate on this subject to satisfy a vain curiosity; we do so in order that we may come to love holy humility, the fundamental virtue of Christianity, by learning of God's love for it. The Son of God became man so that his Father might see in him a submissive and obedient God.

Let us see how much God loves humility.

O divine act of obedience by which Jesus Christ began his life, new sacrifice of a submissive God, in what temple will you be offered to the eternal Father? Where shall we see for the first time the marvelous spectacle of a humiliated and obedient God? It will be in the womb of the Blessed Virgin. This will be the temple; this will be the altar on which Jesus will consecrate to his Father his first vows of obedience.

And how does it come to be, O divine Savior, that you should choose this Virgin to be the sacred temple in which you will adore your heavenly Father with such profound humility? It is because this divine temple is founded on and sanctified by humility. The Word, emptied and abased, willed that humility should prepare his temple. There was no fit dwelling place in the world for him except within the one that had been consecrated by humility.

The angel Gabriel announced to Mary that she would conceive the Son of the Most High, the King

The Humility of God

and Liberator of Israel. Who would think that a woman would be troubled by such good news? Could she receive a more glorious hope or a more magnificent promise on better authority? An angel told her of it on God's behalf. Nevertheless, Mary was troubled. She was afraid. She hesitated.

Then she replied: "How can this be, since I have no husband?" (Luke 1:34). She was anxious for the purity of her virginity. If I should conceive the Son of the Most High, it would truly be a great glory for me, but what shall become of my holy virginity? I cannot consent to lose it. O marvelous purity, you are not only proof against all human promises, but also against the promises of God! For what do you wait, O Divine Word and chaste lover of pure souls? When shall you come to earth, if this purity does not attract you? But you must wait, for your temple has not yet received its finishing touch. The angel responds to Mary, "The Holy Spirit will come upon you" (Luke 1:35). He *will* come — that is, he has not yet come.

Let us now attend to the Blessed Virgin's next words: "Behold, I am the handmaid of the Lord; let it be to me according to your word" (Luke 1:38). It is apparent that her humility is speaking here; this is the language of obedience. Mary does not exalt herself in her new dignity as Mother of God. She does not allow herself to be transported by joy; she declares only her submission. And immediately the heavens open, torrents of grace fall upon Mary, the floodwaters of the Holy Spirit cover her, and the Word makes himself a body from her most pure blood. "The power of the Most High will overshadow you" (Luke 1:35), and this Son that he eternally engenders in his being he now engenders in the womb of the Blessed Virgin.

How can such a great miracle occur? It is because of your humility, O Blessed Virgin, that you are the first to receive, and within your very self, the One who is destined for the whole world. You become the temple of the Incarnate God, and the humility that fills you has made this dwelling place agreeable to him, so that, by a particular grace, he has willed that for nine whole months you should possess as your very own the common good of the entire universe. How true it is that humility is the source of every grace and that it alone can attract Jesus to us.

If God seems very distant from man or if it seems that his mercy has been withdrawn, it is because humility has been banished from the world. A humble man, a circumspect and modest man: such a one is almost unknown to us. Well then, you proud nothingness, from

The Humility of God

what example will you learn to lower yourself, if God's does not suffice? He has nothing above him, and yet he gave himself a master by becoming man. Yet you, although bound on all sides by chains of dependence, are unable to submit your spirit.

Perhaps you will say in your defense, "I know very well how to bear myself humbly." Do not think it so easy to fool others by a modest appearance. Do you not see that your outward submission has its origin in your pride? Can it not be read in your heart that you humble yourself only in the presence of those admired as great? Your vanity blinds you. Pride must be rooted deep within your heart, for you are able to humble yourself thanks only to your arrogance. Yet this arrogance, which you hide because it threatens to injure your fortunes, will appear in all its force as soon as a little ray of favor shines on you.

Your heart has no more weight than a piece of straw! Sudden prosperity carries you off, and you are no longer even recognizable. How is it that you have so quickly forgotten the mud from which you came and all your many weaknesses?

Return, O proud one, to your own nothingness and learn from the Blessed Virgin not to let yourself be dazzled by the brilliance and pleasure of unexpected good news. The high dignity of the Mother of God led her only to humble herself the more. Yet this abasement brought her glory. God, delighted by so profound a humility, came and humbled himself in her womb.

8

The Gospel Embraces the Law

Although it may seem that the Gospel and the Law are so distant as to be almost opposed, in truth there is nothing more united, for Christ came into the world to fulfill the Law and the prophets by the truth of his Gospel. In the Law there is neither a word nor a syllable that does not find its true meaning in Jesus Christ alone, and Jesus never took a single step other than those that accomplished exactly and point by point what was written of him in the Law. Whatever the differences that seem to separate them, Moses and Jesus stand side by side; the synagogue and the Church hold each other's hands; and in the visit that Mary paid to Elizabeth and in their embrace, it is the Gospel that kisses the Law, the Church that embraces the synagogue.

The first thing to note in this portrait of the Gospel embracing the Law, of Mary greeting St. Elizabeth, is the vast difference in age between the two cousins. The

Meditations on Mary

Gospel portrays Elizabeth in an extreme old age, and Mary in the bloom of youth. In the age of Elizabeth we see the feebleness of the Law as it dies, and in the youth of the Blessed Virgin, the eternal newness of the Church. The youth of the Church is such that time can neither change her nor acquire any rights over her. Eternal things do not grow old, while, on the contrary, perishable things tend ineluctably toward their end and consequently are always aging. That is why the apostle, speaking of the Law, said, "[W]hat is becoming obsolete and growing old is ready to vanish away" (Heb. 8:13). Thus, the synagogue was always aging, because one day it would be abolished. The Christian Church never ages, because she will live forever. The end of the world will not be a limit to her duration; then she will cease to exist on earth, but she will begin to reign in heaven. She will be not extinguished but transferred to a glorious place, where she will remain always in the bloom of perpetual youth.

We ought to rejoice, for if we grow old in this world according to our animal nature, the Church, by whom we have a spiritual nature, never ages. It is therefore with good reason that Elizabeth represents the synagogue, soon to fall, while Mary, in the bloom of youth, represents the Church of Jesus Christ, forever young, forever strong, forever vigorous. Then, inasmuch as the spirit of

The Gospel Embraces the Law

Christianity is a spirit of newness and youthfulness, let us "cleanse out the old leaven," as the apostle said (1 Cor. 5:7). We must not allow our zeal to grow old but must keep it ever young and ardent.

If we wish to live according to the spiritual youthfulness of the law of grace, we must always be inebriated with the wine of the new covenant that Jesus promised to his faithful in the kingdom of God his Father, that is to say, in the Church. It is the Savior himself who compared the spirit of the New Law to new wine. This was so that we would understand that just as new wine cleanses itself by its own power, so also we should preserve the new spirit of Christianity in its strength and fervor, so that it can chase off all our sins and that lazy coldness that makes us slow and benumbed in works of piety.

Mary represents the Church for us not only by her age but also by her perpetual virginity. Marriage is sacred and to be "held in honor among all" (Heb. 13:4). Yet if we compare it to holy virginity, we must admit that marriage savors of nature, virginity of grace. And if we consider attentively what the apostle said about marriage and virginity, we will find a portrait of the synagogue and the Church. The former is "anxious about worldly affairs" (1 Cor. 7:33), for that was the end of the synagogue, which had for its portion "the dew of heaven and the fatness of the earth" (Gen. 27:28). It had only earthly promises, promises of a land flowing in milk and honey. What of virginity? It is "anxious about the affairs of the Lord" (1 Cor. 7:34). This is the purpose of holy Church, which looks "not to the things that are seen but to the things that are unseen" (2 Cor. 4:18).

We see, then, a prefiguring of the Church in the Blessed Virgin, and an image of the synagogue in Elizabeth. This most pure Virgin was married, and it is by her divine marriage that she represents the Church. For, as St. Augustine taught, Joseph and Mary were not joined by physical attraction, rather, they had no bond other than the faith that they pledged to one another, and that is also what joins the Church to her Spouse, Jesus Christ. The faith of Jesus is pledged to the Church, and that of the Church to Jesus: "I will betroth you to me in faithfulness" (Hos. 2:20).

It is remarkable that in spite of living with her husband, Elizabeth is said to have been sterile. Mary, on the contrary, made a promise of perpetual virginity, but the Scriptures, which never lie, show her to have been fertile. Here we see the sterility of the synagogue, which by its own power was unable to give birth to children of heaven, and the divine fertility of the Church, of which it is written, "Rejoice, O barren one that dost not bear"

The Gospel Embraces the Law

(Gal. 4:27). Nevertheless, the sterile woman gives birth, and Elizabeth has a son just as the Blessed Virgin does; similarly the synagogue gave birth, but to prefiguring and prophecy. Elizabeth conceived, but she conceived a precursor to Jesus, a voice that made straight the way. Mary gave birth to Truth itself.

Let us admire the worthiness of the Virgin and of the Church in their similarity. God begets his Son in eternity by an ineffable generation, as far removed from flesh and blood as the life of God is separated from mortal life. This only-begotten Son, born from all eternity, will be born in time. Will it come to pass in a carnal manner? Banish such sacrilegious thoughts! His generation in time had to be a most pure image of his chaste generation in eternity. Only the eternal Father could cause Mary to bear his own Son; inasmuch as this Son would have something in common with God, it was necessary that God give to her his proper fertility. To give birth to the Son of God could not be the result of natural fertility; it required a divine fertility.

O the incredible dignity of Mary! We should imitate her purity, which represents so perfectly that of the Church.

9

Gratitude for Grace

Sent into the world to be its light, Jesus Christ began to teach men from the moment of his coming. While still in the womb of the Blessed Virgin, without a word and, it seems, without any movement, he spoke. He is the Word of the eternal Father, and so it is not only all that he does and all that he suffers that speaks, but also all that he is, and in a manner that those who are attuned to the divine mysteries can understand. St. John the Baptist understood him and leapt for joy. Jesus' mute eloquence was able to move the heart of a child still in the womb. Let us be attentive to this preaching that does not strike our ears but speaks so powerfully to our spirit.

We have seen that Elizabeth is an image of the Law and the Blessed Virgin of the Church; now we see them meet. They are cousins, which shows us that the Old Law and the New Law are closely related, that they both belong to the same heavenly family. Yet it does not suffice that they be related; they must embrace. When Jesus has accomplished the prophecies, when he has been offered up, have not the Old Law and the New Law embraced in him?

We see this clearly in the person of St. John the Baptist. As St. Augustine tells us, St. John is like the dawn of a new day, which is neither nighttime nor day but the border at which they meet. St. John joined the synagogue to the Church. He is the ambassador of the synagogue, who welcomes Jesus as the Liberator. He is also the ambassador of God, who introduces Jesus to the synagogue. Jesus embraced John when he received baptism from him. John embraced Jesus when he said, "Behold, the Lamb of God" (John 1:29). This is why Jesus comes to John, and Mary to Elizabeth. He is the first to act; it belongs to grace to take the initiative.

Grace is never given to us because we have done good works, but rather so that we may do them. Grace is so much in harmony with our best desires that it anticipates them. Grace extends throughout our entire lives, and, over the course of our lives, it always remains grace. The good use that we make of graces draws forth more of them, yet they do not cease to be grace: "grace for grace" (John 1:16). It never shows itself to be what it is — that is, grace — more than when it comes to us unlooked for:

as when Mary comes to St. Elizabeth and when Jesus comes to St. John the Baptist.

We see how Jesus anticipates his precursor; we must also see how he takes the initiative in the life of grace. Our zeal for the salvation of souls is the sign that we have been called. Jesus comes to John, the liberator to the captive. Jesus visits John, because the physician must go to visit the sick. Yet Jesus is in the womb, and so is John: it seems that the physician is just as infirm as the patient. Jesus has taken on our infirmities in order to provide the remedy. In a similar way, it is our duty to make ourselves weak with the weak in order to cure them. "Who is weak, and I am not weak?" asks the apostle. "Who is made to fall, and I am not indignant?" (2 Cor. 11:29). If we wish to know just how far the apostle descended in order to make himself weak with the weak, we must remember that he lowered himself to the point of giving milk to children: "We were gentle among you, like a nurse taking care of her children" (1 Thess. 2:7). Just as a nurse or a mother kneels down to be near the child and modulates her voice, departing from her normal way of speaking so that the child will be comforted, so also should we dispose of our eloquence in the service of our neighbor.

Mary and Elizabeth embrace and greet one another. The Law honors the gospel by predicting it; the gospel

Gratitude for Grace

honors the Law by fulfilling it: this is their mutual greeting. Let us listen to their holy conversation. "Blessed are you among women" (Luke 1:42). O Church, O society of the faithful, assembly blessed among all those of the earth: you are singularly blessed because you were uniquely chosen. "My dove, my perfect one, is only one" (Song of Sol. 6:9). "Blessed is she who believed" (Luke 1:45), said Elizabeth to Mary, and with good reason, for faith is the source of all graces. "My righteous one shall live by faith" (Heb. 10:38). "There would be a fulfillment of what was spoken ... from the Lord" (Luke 1:45). Everything will be accomplished: behold the Christian life.

Christians are children of the promise, children of hope: this is the testimony that the synagogue gives to the Church. The Church does not disavow the gifts or advantages she has received; on the contrary, she acknowledges them: "he who is mighty has done great things for me" (Luke 1:49). She gives praise to God: "My soul magnifies the Lord" (Luke 1:46). Thus, in this admirable encounter of the synagogue with the Church, whereas the synagogue, according to its duty, bears witness to the Church, the Church, for her part, bears witness to divine mercy, so that we may learn that the true sacrifice of the New Law is a sacrifice of thanksgiving. Accordingly, we

Meditations on Mary

are admonished in the celebration of the holy mysteries to give thanks to the Lord our God.

We must therefore confess that we are a work of mercy: our sacrifice is Eucharistic, a sacrifice of thanksgiving. This was the sacrifice offered by St. John. In leaping for joy, he gave thanks to the Liberator. If the Liberator caused John to leap for joy by means of his presence alone, what will it be like in heaven when we shall see him face-to-face? John was in his mother's womb and was able to sense Jesus, who was in his Mother's womb. Jesus comes to our very selves, yet we seem to be unaware that he is with us.

10

The Magnificat

It was in the chaste delight of a holy peace that the Blessed Virgin rejoiced in our Lord and said: "My soul magnifies the Lord, and my spirit rejoices in God my Savior" (Luke 1:46–47). It is certain that her soul was at peace, for she was in possession of Jesus Christ.

Her song can be divided into three parts. Mary first tells us about the favors that God has shown to her: "He has regarded the low estate of his handmaiden; he has done great things for me." Then she tells how the glory of the world has been cast down: "he has scattered the proud; he has put down the mighty; the rich he has sent empty away." Finally she concludes her sacred canticle by admiring God's truthfulness and fidelity to his promises: "He has helped his servant Israel, in remembrance of his mercy, as he spoke to our fathers" (cf. Luke 1:48–55). At first sight these three things do not seem to have much to do with one another. Together, however, they are most admirable: it seems that the intention of the Blessed Virgin was to inspire the hearts of the faithful with a love of the peace God had given her.

To show us the sweetness of that peace, she first reveals its principle: God's regard for the just, his goodness toward them, and his providence that watches over them. "He has regarded the low estate of his handmaiden" (Luke 1:48). This is what gives peace to holy souls. Yet because the brilliance of the world's favors and vain attractions could turn them away from the godly things, she then shows us the world cast down and its glory destroyed, annihilated. Finally, as this overturning of human greatness and the complete happiness of faithful souls does not appear to us in this world, she strengthens our spirits in the peace of God by noting the credibility of his promises.

Tell us, O divine Virgin, tell us what makes your soul rejoice in God. It is because he has looked upon me; "he has regarded the low estate of his handmaiden." We must understand what the regard of God signifies and imagine the benefits that it contains. We note in the Scriptures that the regard of God signifies his favor and benevolence, his help and protection. When God regards the just with his favor, he looks upon them like a good father who is always ready to listen to their requests: "The eyes of the Lord are toward the righteous, and his ears toward

The Magnificat

their cry" (Ps. 34:15). The same prophet explains to us, in another psalm, the regard of protection: "Behold, the eye of the Lord is on those who fear him, on those who hope in his steadfast love, that he may deliver their soul from death, and keep them alive in famine" (Ps. 33:18–19). By this regard God watches over men and women of goodwill to protect them from the evils that menace them. That is why David adds: "Our soul waits for the Lord; he is our help and shield" (Ps. 33:20). How could a soul assured of this twofold regard fail to be at peace?

It is the Blessed Virgin who has been singularly honored by this twofold regard of providence: God looked upon her with an eye of favor when he preferred her to all other women, as well as to the angels, the seraphim, and to every other creature. The regard of protection watched over her when he preserved her from the corruption of sin, the fires of concupiscence, and all the spiritual ills that afflict our nature. This is why her song is so full of joy. Note how she celebrates God's favor: "He who is mighty has done great things for me" (Luke 1:49). He has filled me with his graces. Yet see also how she praises his protection: "He has shown strength with his arm" (Luke 1:51). He has filled me with his graces and has done things for me so great that no creature can do their equal, nor any intellect comprehend them. Yet, if he has opened his generous hands to fill my soul with good things, he has also been pleased to extend his arm to keep away every evil. It is Mary he favored by these two regards of benevolence and protection, "for he has regarded the low estate of his handmaiden."

Christian souls: you also have been honored, and this should give your souls peace. Yes, certainly, children of God, he looks upon you with benevolence; he reveals to you his kindly countenance. Of course, his face is terrifying to us when a guilty conscience reproaches us with the horror of our sins and makes God appear to us as a judge, and an angry one. Yet when, in the course of a good life, he causes a certain serenity to arise in our conscience, he then shows an amiable and tranquil face; he calms every trouble and chases away every cloud. The faithful who hope in him no longer think of him as a judge: instead we see him as a good father whose sweet invitation fills us with confidence: "I will say to God, thou art my support" (Ps. 41:9; Douay-Rheims), and it seems that God responds, "I am your deliverance" (Ps. 35:3). We then enjoy perfect peace, because we are covered by the hand of God, and from whatever quarter threats should come, a voice from the heart strengthens and assures us: "If God is for us, who is against us?" (Rom. 8:31). "The Lord is my light and my salvation; whom shall I fear? The Lord

The Magnificat

is the stronghold of my life; of whom shall I be afraid?" (Ps. 27:1).

Such is the hidden peace that God gives to his servants, a peace that the world cannot understand and that, exiled from the world by its continual tumult, seems to thrive only in retirement and solitude. It is disdain for the world that appears next in the canticle, disdain for the false peace that it promises and the vanities for which it would have us pine. Let us see the world for what it is: something of little account. We see all human grandeur overthrown, the proud struck down to the earth. In this great overturning of human things, nothing seems more exalted than the simple and humble of heart. This is why we should say with Mary, "He has put down the mighty from their thrones, and exalted those of low degree" (Luke 1:52).

To enter into this sentiment, we must reflect on the strange opposition between God and the world. All of the things that God lifts up, the world would cast down; all that the world esteems, God would destroy and confound. We see this by experience. Who are those favored by God? The humble, the modest, the circumspect. Who are those put forward by the world? The bold and adventuresome. God favors the pure of heart and the sincere. The world prefers the crafty and the unscrupulous. The

Meditations on Mary

world requires violence of those who would carry off its favors. God gives his favors only to the self-controlled, and there is nothing greater before God or useless according to the world than the temperance in which virtue consists. Here is the struggle between Jesus Christ and the world: what the one raises up, the other casts down. This battle will last until the end of time.

The world can be considered in two ways: by looking to its present goods or by setting our sights on the last judgment. To those who look for present goods, the world gives advantages, and they imagine themselves to be victorious, because God, who is patient, allows them to enjoy a momentary shadow of happiness. They see those who are in high estate and admire their luxury. They are blind judges and hasty. Should we not wait for the battle's end before declaring the victor? The hand of God is coming, and it will break them like a clay pot.

This is what the Blessed Virgin sees, and with her the children of God who enjoy the sweetness of his peace. They see that the world is at war with God, but they see that the two armies are not equal. They do not allow themselves to be dazzled by the apparent advantages that God allows the children of this world to enjoy. They consider the justice of God that is to come. This is why they laugh at the world's glory, and amid the pomp of its

The Magnificat

triumph, they sing of its defeat. They say not only that God will cast down the proud, but that he has already done so; they say not only that he will depose the powerful, but that they are already at his feet, trembling and astonished by their fall. And as for you, O rich of this world, who imagine yourselves to have your fill of good things, you will find yourselves poor and your hands empty; your riches will stream away like water: "the rich he has sent empty away" (Luke 1:53). Here is worldly grandeur cast down, and God triumphant and victorious. What joy for his children, to see their enemies fallen at their feet, and his humble servants with their heads held high!

Let us sing this holy song, the true song of those who have set the world at naught. Let us sing the world's defeat, the destruction of all human pride and wealth. And you, who sigh after wealth, who think nothing great that does not turn a profit, and nothing pleasant that does not taste of riches: why do you think this way? Are you not children of God? Do you not carry the mark of his adoption, the sacred character of baptism? Is not the earth a place of exile? Is not heaven your home? Why do you so much admire the world? If you are from Jerusalem, why are you singing songs of Babylon? All that you say and think about the world is said in a foreign language learned during your exile. Forget that foreign language;

Meditations on Mary

learn to speak the language of your home. Do not call happy those whom you see enjoying the world's pleasures. Those whose God is the Lord are truly happy.

With these thoughts, console yourself and live in peace. Learn from the Blessed Virgin that the Lord has looked upon you, and assured of his unshakeable support, do not be dazzled by the wealth of this world. Look upon it as already cast down. If the time of exile seems too long to you, think about the faithfulness of his promises: "as he spoke to our fathers, to Abraham and to his posterity forever" (Luke 1:55). What he spoke to Abraham he brought to pass two thousand years later by sending his Messiah. The rest he will bring to pass in good time, and we will see the day of everlasting happiness he has promised to us. Amen.

11

Bethlehem

Such trials God prepares for holy souls! When Joseph thought himself obliged to abandon as faithless the one whom he had chosen as the purest of virgins, he was about to do what would be fatal both to the mother's purity and the child's life. He could not be unaware that the Blessed Virgin was with child, and what could he think but that it had come about naturally? For it would not have occurred to any man to suppose the truth, to imagine a kind of miracle God had never before performed.

He was "a just man" (Matt. 1:19), and his justice would require him to quit the company of one whom he could not regard as innocent. He was doing the best that could be hoped when he "resolved to send her away quietly" (Matt. 1:19). If he had given in to jealousy, which is as "cruel as the grave" (Song of Sol. 8:6), what might he not have done? Under a law of inflexible rigor, there was no limit to what his vengeance might have exacted, and his very justice would have fanned the flames of his passion. Yet Jesus had begun to pour out his spirit of meekness upon the world, and he shared it with the one whom he had chosen to serve as his father.

The most moderate and equitable of men, Joseph never even considered the most extreme course of action. He wished only to take leave secretly of one whom he could no longer accept blamelessly. And yet what sorrow was his to think that he had been deceived in his trust for her chastity and virtue. To lose the one he loved, and to leave her a helpless prey to calumny and public outcry! God could have spared him this misery by revealing the mystery to him earlier, but then his virtue would not have been put to the test prepared for him. Nor would we have seen Joseph's victory over the most indomitable of all passions, and the most righteous jealousy that ever existed would not have been trampled underfoot by his virtue.

In the same events we see Mary's faith. She saw the suffering of her spouse and understood all the consequences of her holy child-bearing, yet without appearing to be anxious, without daring to enlighten her spouse or to reveal heaven's secret; she knew the risk of seeing herself mistrusted and abandoned, or perhaps lost and condemned. She left everything in God's hands and remained at peace.

Bethlehem

These were the circumstances in which an angel of the Lord was sent to Joseph and said to him: "Joseph, son of David, do not fear to take Mary your wife, for that which is conceived in her is of the Holy Spirit" (Matt. 1:20). How calm are those words. What astonishment and what humility were Joseph's! If we are to have any understanding at all of these things, it is for God alone to give it to us.

"She will bear a son, and you shall call his name Jesus" (Matt. 1:21). Why "you"? You are not the father. He has no father but God. But God has transferred his rights to you. You will stand as a father to Jesus Christ. Formed by the Holy Spirit in the womb of the one who belongs to you, he also belongs to you. With the authority and rights of a father, then, have also a father's heart toward Jesus. God, "who fashions the hearts of all" (Ps. 33:15), today places a father's heart in you. How blessed are you, for at the same time he gives Jesus the heart of a son toward you. You are the true spouse of his holy Mother; you share with her this beloved Son and the graces that flow from his love. Go then and at the proper time name the child, giving him the name Jesus—both for you and for us—so that he will be our Savior as well as yours.

After his dream and the angel's words, Joseph was a changed man. He became a father and a husband in his heart. The effect of his marriage was the tender care that he had for Mary and the divine Child. He began this blessed ministry by traveling to Bethlehem, and we know all that followed from it.

What is it that you do, you princes of the earth, who set all the world in motion to perform an accounting of the subjects of your empire? You wish to know their productivity, their revenue, and the size of the army that can be assembled, and so you declare a census. This was what you thought you were doing. Yet God had other plans, which you were carrying out without having any idea of it. His Son must be born in Bethlehem, David's humble home. He had made his prophet predict it seven hundred years before (cf. Mic. 5:2), and now the whole world is bestirred so that the prophecy may be fulfilled.

When they were in Bethlehem — to obey the prince but also to obey the order of God — "the time came for her to be delivered" (Luke 2:6), and Jesus, the Son of David, was born in Bethlehem, "the village where David was" (John 7:42). The public registers attested his origin. The Roman Empire bore witness to the royal lineage of Jesus Christ, and Caesar, unknowingly, carried out the orders of God.

Let us also be enrolled at Bethlehem. Bethlehem, the house of bread. Let us go there to taste the bread of

Bethlehem

heaven, the bread of angels become human food. Let us consider all our churches to be true Bethlehems, true homes of the bread of life. This is the bread that God gives to the poor in the birth of Jesus. If with him they love poverty and come to adore him in the manger, then they shall find true wealth, then the "poor shall eat and be satisfied" (Ps. 22:26).

12

Wonder

Jesus' first act upon coming into the world was to devote himself to God and to accomplish his will. This he did in his Mother's womb by the disposition of his heart; then by presenting himself in the Temple, by letting himself be handed over to the Lord as something belonging to him.

"Now there was a man in Jerusalem, whose name was Simeon, and this man was righteous and devout, looking for the consolation of Israel, and the Holy Spirit was upon him. And it had been revealed to him by the Holy Spirit that he should not see death before he had seen the Lord's Christ. And inspired by the Spirit he came into the temple" at the very moment when "the parents brought in the child Jesus" (Luke 2:25–27). It was a happy encounter, but not a chance one. In truth there are no coincidences, for all is governed by a wisdom whose infinite capacity embraces the very least of circumstances. Jesus

Wonder

was brought to the Temple by his parents, and Simeon was directed there by a special order of God.

"And his father and his mother marveled at what was said about him" (Luke 2:33). Let us attempt to understand their wonder. It is an intimate passion of the soul that, pierced and overcome by the size, splendor, and majesty of the things it beholds, after perhaps some effort to express itself at that level, at last recognizes that it cannot even understand the incomprehensibility of the thing believed. Even the most exalted thoughts of our minds are entirely unworthy of God. Fearing to degrade its thoughts by attempting to express them, the soul remains in silence before God, unable to say a word, unless the words of David. "O LORD, our Lord, how majestic is thy name in all the earth! Thou whose glory above the heavens is chanted" (Ps. 8:1). Or those of Solomon: "Behold, heaven and the highest heaven cannot contain thee" (1 Kings 8:27). It belongs to you alone to praise you. And so my soul is bewildered and confused, and remains silent before your face. My amazement turns to love, but a love that senses that we are unable to love you adequately, and so plunges itself in your immense greatness, as into a bottomless abyss.

Let us return to Joseph and Mary. They "marveled at what was said about him." They knew more about him than those who were speaking of him. Why did they wonder? It is true that the angel had not told them that he would be the Savior of the nations. Mary had only heard about the throne of David and that "he will reign over the house of Jacob" (Luke 1:33). She had nevertheless sensed with an altogether prophetic instinct that "all generations will call me blessed" (Luke 1:48). This seems to comprehend all people as well as every age. And the adoration of the Magi was a prefiguring of the conversion of the Gentiles. Be that as it may, Simeon was the first who seems to have declared that Jesus would be the light to the nations, and that gave them great cause to wonder.

The Holy Spirit wishes us to understand an excellent way of honoring mysteries without laboring to discover their causes, which is to remain before God in wonder and silence. In this kind of prayer, there is no question of formulating thoughts, nor of making great efforts. We are in the presence of God. We marvel at the graces he has given to us. And we say a hundred times without saying a word: "[W]hat is man that thou are mindful of him, and the son of man that thou dost care for him?" (Ps. 8:4). Once again: what is man that you, most admirable Lord, should wish to think about him? We plunge into wonder and gratitude, not attempting to pronounce the least

Wonder

word — either spoken or thought — as long as this blessed and recollected disposition should remain.

In this wonder there is a submissive ignorance that, content to be shown God's grandeur, does not ask to know any more and, lost in the incomprehensibility of his mysteries, looks upon them with an interior stillness that is equally disposed to see or not to see, to see more or less according to God's good pleasure. Love's first effect is to make us admire what we love and always look upon it with pleasure, bring our eyes back to it, and not want to lose sight of it. This manner of honoring God may be seen in the saints from the earliest days, as in the case of David, when he says, "[W]hat is man?" and "[H]ow majestic is thy name in all the earth!" (Ps. 8:4, 9). It is the song of the saints in heaven: "Who shall not fear and glorify thy name, O Lord? For thou alone art holy" (Rev. 15:4). Afterward there is silence, because we do not know how to express our tenderness, our respect, our joy — that is, all that we sense when in the presence of God — and "there was silence in heaven for about half an hour" (Rev. 8:1). It is a marvelous silence, which cannot last long in this turbulent and tumultuous life.

13

The Flight to Egypt

After "they had performed everything according to the law of the Lord, they returned into Galilee, to their own city, Nazareth" (Luke 2:39). This passage from St. Luke suggests that the Blessed Virgin and St. Joseph remained with the Child in Bethlehem or nearby, and close to Jerusalem, until they had accomplished all that they would do in the Temple. It was a long walk from there to Nazareth, whence they had come and where their dwelling lay, and it was only natural that to avoid repeating the journey they should have remained in the vicinity.

St. Luke does not tell us what happened prior to the departure; St. Matthew had already recorded it. This Evangelist tells of the adoration of the Magi, their return home by another route, the angel's warning to Joseph, the flight to Egypt, the fury of Herod and the massacre of the Holy Innocents, a second message from the angel after the death of Herod—all of which seem to follow

The Flight to Egypt

the Savior's birth in rapid succession—and then a third message from heaven to settle them in Nazareth.

The time was short. The Holy Family was hidden, while Herod awaited news of the Child from the Magi, whom he believed would tell him the Child's whereabouts. It was to be expected that he should have to wait a few days to hear from them. During those few days, Joseph and Mary were able to take the child to the Temple without being discovered. The wonders that transpired there could have awakened Herod's jealousy, but they were promptly followed by the flight to Egypt. Thus are the leaders of this world always the playthings of God, who turns their plans in the direction he chooses.

After the Magi had departed, God saw such cruel dispositions in the heart of Herod that he foiled him by sending a message by his holy angel to Joseph as he slept: "Rise, take the child and his mother, and flee to Egypt ... for Herod is about to search for the child, to destroy him" (Matt. 2:13). Was there no way to save him other than by this hurried flight? God did not will that all his purposes should be accomplished through miracles. It often belongs to his providence to follow the ordinary course of nature, which comes from him just as much as do extraordinary events. The Son of God "himself is beset with weakness" (Heb. 5:2). To conform to this condition, he subjected himself voluntarily to the common happenings of human life, and by the same dispensation according to which he was hidden during the course of his ministry, he was now hidden so as to frustrate the secret designs of his enemies.

Wherever Jesus comes, he comes with his Cross and with all the contradictions that must accompany it. "Rise, take the child and his mother, and flee to Egypt." We must weigh all of these words and recognize that they inspire fear in us. "Rise," do not delay for a moment. He does not say "go," but instead "flee." The angel himself seems to be alarmed by the danger to the child. Why, unless it is to put to the test the love and fidelity of Joseph? He must have been moved by seeing the danger to his dear wife and Son.

It is a strange condition for this poor artisan suddenly banished for no other reason than that he has custody of Jesus. Before the Child's birth, he and his holy spouse lived in poverty, but in peace, quietly earning their bread by the work of their hands. As soon as Jesus is given to them, they have no more rest. Nevertheless, Joseph remains submissive and does not complain about the trouble the Child brings, trouble that is nothing less than persecution. He departs. He goes to Egypt, where he has no place to live, without knowing when he will return to

The Flight to Egypt

his homeland, his workshop, or his modest home. We do not gain Jesus without partaking of his Cross.

Christian fathers and mothers: learn that your children will be crosses for you. Do not stint with the care that they need, not only to preserve their lives, but for what is their true preservation, which is to raise them in virtue. Prepare yourselves for the crosses that God makes ready for you in these proofs of your mutual love. And after having offered them to God as Joseph and Mary did, be ready, like them, to receive, in one way or another, more suffering than sweetness.

14

The Holy Family

Jesus Christ did not wish to be born into a wealthy family, nor to choose parents who were illustrious for their learning. He was content with their piety. Following his example, let us rejoice not in the brilliance of our family, but in its good examples and edifying behavior, and that it is a true school of religion where we learn to fear God and to serve him.

Joseph and Mary, according to the precept of the Law, went to Jerusalem "every year at the feast of the Passover" (Luke 2:41). They took with them their dear Son, always submissive to his mortal parents, who allowed himself to be instructed by this holy observance. He was, of course, there before they took him, for he was the very basis of the feast, the true lamb who would be sacrificed and consumed in memory of our passage to the next life. One year at the feast, Jesus made it known that his submission did not stem from the infirmity of his youth, but instead from

The Holy Family

a more profound source. To accomplish this mystery, he chose the age of twelve years, an age at which children become capable of sound reasoning. This he did so as not to appear to have left nature behind, but instead to have followed its normal course.

Jesus' abandonment of his holy Mother and St. Joseph was not a punishment of them, but instead a trial. We do not read that they left him from negligence or because of some other fault; it was, therefore, for the sake of their humiliation. Jesus left them when it pleased him to do so; "we do not know whence he comes or whither he goes" (cf. John 3:8). He passed "through the midst of them" and "went away" (Luke 4:30), and they did not know it. The holy Child had disappeared, and they were anxious and sorrowful, for they did not find him "among their kinsfolk and acquaintances" (Luke 2:44). How many times did St. Joseph reproach himself for his carelessness with his sacred trust? Who is not touched to the quick with him, and with the most tender Mother and best spouse who ever lived?

His parents were astonished to find him "in the temple, sitting among the teachers" (Luke 2:46). This shows that they had hitherto seen nothing extraordinary about his life, for everything had been veiled under the shadows of childhood. And Mary, who was the first to be aware of the loss of her dear son, was also the first to complain about his absence. "Son, why have you treated us so? Behold, your father and I have been looking for you anxiously" (Luke 2:48). We note that she said "your father and I": she called St. Joseph his father, for indeed he was, not only by his adoption of the holy child, but also by sentiment, by his care for him, and through the sorrow that made Mary say, "Your father and I have been looking for you anxiously." They were joined in their affliction, because although Joseph did not have any part in his birth, he nevertheless felt the joy of having Jesus and the sorrow of losing him. An obedient and respectful wife, Mary named Joseph first: "your father and I," and paid him the honor of speaking of him like any other father. O Jesus, how well-ordered was everything in your family life.

"And he went down with them and came to Nazareth" (Luke 2:51). We must not lose a single word of this holy text; the Evangelist says that he "went down" with them to Nazareth. After having strayed for a while to do the work of his Father, he returned to his ordinary conduct, to the ways of his parents, to obedience. And this is perhaps, in a mystical mode, what accounts for the phrase "he went down," but in any case it is true that he placed himself between their hands until his baptism, that is,

The Holy Family

until the age of almost thirty years, and did nothing other than obey them.

We should be astonished by the word: was that then the whole work of Jesus Christ, the Son of God? His entire duty was to obey two of his creatures. With regard to what did he obey them? In the lowest of activities, in the practice of a mechanical art? Who are they who weep and complain when the work they are assigned does not correspond to their talents, or rather to their pride? Let them come to the home of Joseph and Mary, and let them see Jesus at work there. We do not ever read that his parents had domestic servants; like other poor folk, they had only their children, their Child, to serve them. Jesus himself said that he came "to serve" (Matt. 20:28). When he went to the desert, the angels were obliged to come and serve him, for we never see him with servants at his beck and call. What is known is that he himself worked in his father's workshop (cf. Matt. 13:55).

And there is considerable evidence to suggest that he lost his father well before the time of his ministry. At his Passion, he left his Mother in the care of his Beloved Disciple, who received her into his home, which would not have happened if Joseph had still been alive. From the beginning of his ministry, we see Mary together with Jesus at the wedding feast at Cana, but there is no mention of

Meditations on Mary

Joseph. A little while later, we see him go to Capernaum with his Mother, his brethren, and his disciples (see John 2:12), and Joseph is not named. Mary often appears elsewhere, but after what is said about Jesus' education under the guidance of St. Joseph, we do not again hear about this holy man. This is why at the beginning of his ministry, when he comes to speak in his own country, the people said, "Is not this the carpenter, the son of Mary?" (Mark 6:3). We see him, without shame, supporting a widowed Mother by his own labor and undertaking the petty commerce of his trade that allowed the two of them to live. "Is not his mother called Mary? And are not his brethren James and Joseph and Simon and Judas?" (Matt. 13:55). They do not speak of his father, because, it seems, he had already died. Jesus Christ served him during his final illness.

Happy the father who had such a son to close his eyes! Truly, he died in his arms and, as it were, with a kiss from the Lord. Jesus stayed with his Mother to console her, to serve her: this was the whole of his employment.

O God, what a moving spectacle! O Pride: down on your knees! Jesus, the son of a carpenter, a carpenter himself, was known by his trade, without anything else being said about him. During the early days of the Church, the memory of carts that he had made was kept alive; the

The Holy Family

tradition of them is preserved among the earliest authors. Let then those who live by such an art be consoled and rejoice: Jesus is one of them. Let them learn from him to praise God while they work, to sing psalms and holy songs, and let them know that God will bless their work, and they will be like other Christs.

There have been those who have been ashamed to see the Savior at this kind of work, and they would have had him working miracles from his earliest youth. Such tales they tell of the miracles he wrought in Egypt! Yet all of this exists only in the apocryphal books. The Gospel sums up thirty years of the life of Jesus in these words: "and he was obedient to them" (Luke 2:51), together with these: "the carpenter, the son of Mary." In the obscurity of St. John the Baptist there is something more imposing, for he never appeared among men and "he was in the wilderness" (Luke 1:80). Yet Jesus, in so ordinary a life, was in truth known, but by his lowly work alone.

Could he have been any better hidden than he was? What shall we say, what shall we do to praise him? There is in truth nothing for us to do but to admire him in silence.

15

In Her Heart

Those who grow weary of Jesus and are ashamed to see him spend his life in such total obscurity also grow weary of the Blessed Virgin and wish to attribute an endless series of miracles to her. Our duty is to listen to the Gospel: "his mother kept all these things in her heart" (Luke 2:51). The business of Jesus was to devote himself to his craft; the business of Mary was to meditate day and night on the secrets of God.

When she had lost her Son, did she change her occupation? Where do we see her appear in the Acts of the Apostles or in the tradition of the Church? She is named among those who were in the Upper Room and who received the Holy Spirit (Acts 1:14), and this is all that is reported.

Was that not a sufficiently worthy occupation: to keep in her heart all that she had witnessed of her Son? And if the mysteries of his childhood were so sweet a subject

In Her Heart

of contemplation, how much more will she find to think about in the rest of his life!

Mary meditated on Jesus. Mary, who with St. John is the image of the contemplative life, remained in perpetual contemplation, melting, liquefying in love and desire. What does the Church read on the day of her glorious Assumption? The Gospel of Mary, the sister of Lazarus, seated at the Savior's feet and listening to his words (Luke 10:39). In the treasury of the Scriptures, the Church found nothing more suitable for Mary the Mother of God and so borrowed the Gospel of divine contemplation from another Mary.

What then should be said to those who wish all manner of precious things to be declared about the Blessed Virgin? What should be said to those who are not satisfied by humble and perfect contemplation? For this is what satisfied Mary, and also Jesus himself for thirty years. The silence of the Scriptures about this divine Mother is the greatest and most eloquent of praise.

This then is the part for me: Mary "kept these things in her heart." "One thing is needful," and Mary chose the better part, which shall not be taken away from her (cf. Luke 10:42). Human pride, what are you complaining about with all your anxieties? That you are nothing in the world? What kind of figure was Jesus? What kind of figure was Mary? They were the wonder of the world, a spectacle for God and his angels, and what did they do? Of what consequence were they? What sort of name did they have? And you wish to be renowned and celebrated? You know neither Mary nor Jesus. You want a position that will show off your talents, not bury them. But Jesus makes use of you and gives you these talents, for which he tells us that he will demand an account. The talent that is buried with Jesus and hidden in him: is that not lovely enough in his eyes? Go. You are vain, and you are seeking in an activity that you think to be pious and useful only a pasture for your self-love.

I am stranded. I have nothing to do. My work is too lowly for me and brings me no pleasure. I want to leave it behind and to take my family with me. Did Mary and Jesus seek to advance themselves? Look at the divine carpenter with his saw and plane, his tender hands calloused by the use of those rude tools. He stands behind no podium: he would rather exercise a craft that is more humble and more necessary for life. He wields no pen and writes no beautiful words, but he stays at his work and earns his living. He works, he praises, and he blesses the will of God in his humiliation.

And what work did he do on the one occasion when he escaped from the custody of his parents and set himself

In Her Heart

to the affairs of his heavenly Father? He labored for the salvation of men. Yet you say, "I have nothing to do," when in fact the work of the salvation of men is, in part, confided to you. Have you no enemies to reconcile? Quarrels to pacify? Differences to bring to end, so that the Savior can say, "you have gained your brother" (Matt. 18:15)? Is there no wretch who needs to be dissuaded from his complaints, blasphemy, and despair? And should all of these works be taken away from you, will you not still have the work of your own salvation, which for each one of us truly is a work of God? Go to the Temple, if necessary, run away from your mother and father, renounce flesh and blood, and say with Jesus, "We must work the works of him who sent me while it is day" (John 9:4). Let us tremble and humble ourselves if we think nothing in our work worthy of our time.

16

Pierced by a Sword

Let us turn our minds to the desolation of Mary and the bloody wound that pierces her heart. How is a mother's sorrow to be understood? Who can depict such deep emotion? Yet if we attend to her, our hearts will speak to us. We must first recall that just as all the joys of the Blessed Virgin come from being the mother of Jesus Christ, so also does her martyrdom. Her love for him was the source of her agony.

There is no need to call the executioner or to stir up the rage of persecution in order to join this Mother to the sufferings of Jesus. It is true that for the holy martyrs it took the rack, the gibbet, and iron nails to imprint upon their bodies the bloody marks of the crucified Christ. For Mary, all it took was love, and we do not understand her love if we fail to realize that it sufficed to cause her martyrdom. Only one Cross was required for both her beloved son and herself. Eternal Father, did you will for her

Pierced by a Sword

to be covered with wounds? Lead her to the foot of his Cross, and let her love do the rest.

To understand this, we must first reflect upon a mother's love and then lift our thoughts beyond nature to the Blessed Virgin's love. We may see a sort of sketch of what grace did in her heart by noting the marvelous character that nature forms in the hearts of mothers. We cannot admire enough the means employed by nature to achieve its end of uniting mothers to their children. That work begins by attaching children to their mother's womb: nourishment and life are conveyed together. Mother and child run the same risks, and they are, as it were, but one person. Here is a close bond indeed. Should we presume that it comes to an end at birth? No. There is no power that can divide what nature has so well knit together. When the first union comes to an end, another takes its place in the bonds of love and tenderness. The mother carries her child in another way. No sooner has the child come forth from her womb than he is held even closer to her heart.

Let us consider now the eagerness of one mother in the Gospel, the Canaanite whose daughter was tormented by a demon. See her at the Savior's feet, see her tears, hear her cries, and ask yourself whether you can tell who suffers more, the daughter or the mother. "Have

Meditations on Mary

mercy on me, O Lord, Son of David; my daughter is severely possessed by a demon" (Matt. 15:22). She did not say, "Lord, have mercy on my daughter." Instead she said, "Have mercy on me."

But if she wanted mercy for herself, she was speaking of her own suffering. No, she says, I am not speaking of my daughter's torments. Why should I exaggerate my sorrow? If my daughter suffers, then I need mercy. It seems to me as though I were still carrying her in my womb, because when she is tormented, I am troubled to my very depths. Hers is the suffering, but mine is the sorrow. The demon strikes her, but my nature strikes me. We see here the marvelous communication by which a mother is bound to her child, and this suffices for us to understand that Mary's sorrow knows no bounds.

All that we see in the Canaanite woman is but an imperfect shadow of what we should believe in the case of the Blessed Virgin. Her love was incomparably stronger, and although it is impossible for us to comprehend its extent, nevertheless we can have some idea of it if we seek its principle.

Everyone who makes something loves the work he produces. The same principle that brings us to act also causes us to love what we do, so that the same cause that allows a woman to bear a child makes her able to love the child. If we wish to know what cause brought about the maternal love that unites Mary to Jesus, we must consider the origin of her motherhood.

Tell us, O Blessed Virgin, by what power you came to give birth: was it by the power of nature? No. Rather we see that she had vowed herself to a blessed barrenness by her firm resolution to preserve her purity. "How can this be?" she asked, that I should become a mother, I who have resolved to remain a virgin? Listen to what the angel said to her: "the power of the Most High will overshadow you" (Luke 1:34–35). It is manifest that her motherhood came from on high, and consequently so did her love.

How could nature alone have undertaken to form in the Blessed Virgin the love that she should have for her Son? In order to love God worthily, a supernatural principle is required. Did Mary love Jesus as a man or as the man-God? In what manner would she embrace, in the person of Jesus Christ, the divinity and the humanity that the Holy Spirit had bound together? Nature could not have united them, and faith does not allow us to separate them: what then can nature achieve here? Nature urges Mary to love, and she has all that she needs to love a son, but not what is necessary for her to love God. Yet this son and this God are one, so that nature cannot find the means to prompt her to love this Son adequately.

Meditations on Mary

What remains, then, O eternal Father, but for your grace to come and take powerless nature by the hand? It is you who, having communicated your divine fecundity to Mary, made her the Mother of your Son. Now you must bring your work to completion, and having associated her in a certain sense with the chaste generation by which you produce your Word, you now cause to flow in her veins a spark of the infinite love you have for your only-begotten Son, who is the splendor of your glory and the living image of your being.

This is the origin of Mary's love. Accordingly, her affliction is without equal. Nothing can produce a similar effect. Hers is a love that passes the bounds of nature, a tender love, a love that unites because it is born from the very principle of unity. The Father and the Son share the same glory in eternity; the Mother and the Son share the same sufferings, the same flood of bitterness. The Father and the Son share the same throne; the Mother and the Son share the same Cross. If the body of Jesus is broken by blows; Mary also receives the wounds. If his head is pierced with thorns, Mary is rent by their barbs. If he is offered vinegar and gall, Mary swallows all their bitterness. If his body is laid out on the Cross, Mary suffers all the violence. It is love that causes this to be.

Pierced by a Sword

O love, how heavy do you weigh upon her! O love, how you press upon her maternal heart! This love is a weight of iron upon her chest, which binds and oppresses her so violently that it suffocates her and brings her to tears. This love is a burden because it weighs upon Jesus, while Mary suffers alongside him.

Let us meditate on Mary's sorrow and labor to imitate her rather than to understand her. Following her example, let us fill our hearts with the Passion of her Son, so that the abundance of our sorrow will forever close the door upon the joys of this world. Mary could no longer endure life: after the death of her beloved, nothing could please her. It was not for her sake, eternal Father, that the sun was eclipsed: there was already no light for the Virgin. It was not for her sake that you razed the foundations of the Temple, nor that nature should bring forth its horrors: after the death of her Son, everything already seemed to her to be covered with darkness. The figure of this world had passed for her, and, to whichever quarter she turned her eyes, she saw nothing but the shadow of death.

The Cross of Jesus ought to do the same for us. If we share his sorrow, the world should no longer have any pleasures for us. The thorns of the Son of God should have torn out all its bloom, and the bitterness that he was given to drink should render its pleasures insipid.

Meditations on Mary

Happy are they, O Savior, who drink your vinegar and gall. Happy are they to whom your shame has made vanity ridiculous, and who have been so firmly nailed to your Cross that they can lift their arms and hands only to heaven! These are the sentiments that ought to move us at the sight of the Cross of Jesus. Here we ought to draw forth a life-giving sorrow from his wounds, a truly holy sorrow, a fruitful sorrow, which will destroy in us the love of this world, extinguish all its brilliance, and lead us to an eternal mourning for the vanities of our past lives.

17

At the Cross

To appreciate the depths of Mary's resignation, we must note that afflictions can be borne in three ways. We overcome affliction, first and foremost, when the sorrow is entirely dismissed and all sense of it is lost. In this case the passion is entirely appeased, and we are consoled. A second way is when the soul remains stirred and troubled by the evil that it senses, but nevertheless endures it patiently. In this case we are resolved, but still agitated. A third way is when we are sensible of all of the sorrow but are not troubled by it, and it is this case that requires illumination.

In the first of these three conditions, we enjoy perfect peace because the sorrow is gone. In the second, we fight against the sorrow, and although our soul may be victorious, we cannot fail to be agitated by the struggle. In the third case, which does not happen without a miracle in which God gives us great strength, we suffer its violence, but our peace of soul is not lost.

Meditations on Mary

It is with good reason that the Scriptures often compare sorrow to the waves on the ocean. For sorrow has bitter waves that enter into the very depths of our souls: "I have come into deep waters, and the flood sweeps over me" (Ps. 69:2). Our sorrows are impetuous waves that press against us violently: "my calamities have overthrown my feet, and have overwhelmed me with their paths as with waves" (Job 30:12; Douay-Rheims). As with the waves of the sea, just when we think them calmed, they arise again with new fury. Just as Jesus calmed the waters in three ways, so also does God overcome our sorrows.

Sometimes he commanded the water and wind to be calm, after which followed, as the Evangelist says, "a great calm" (Matt. 8:26). Similarly, by pouring out his Spirit upon a troubled soul, he calms it and restores its serenity. For, as St. Paul said, "our bodies had no rest"—he was assaulted by the waves—but "God comforts the downcast" (2 Cor. 7:5–6). Here is God, calming the waves and restoring lost tranquillity. Sometimes he allowed the waters to murmur, he permitted the waves to rise with fierce power, and the boat, tossed violently, risked capsizing. Peter, who was carried upon the waters, feared to be entombed in their depths, but Jesus saved the boat and gave his hand to Peter to support him. Similarly, amid violent troubles, the soul is so agitated that it seems that it

At the Cross

will be swallowed whole: "we were so utterly, unbearably crushed" (2 Cor. 1:8). Nevertheless, Jesus supports us so well that neither the winds nor the storms carry us away: "but that was to make us rely not on ourselves but on God who raises the dead" (2 Cor. 1:9). This is the second case. In the third—the noblest and most glorious—Jesus let go the tempest's reins and allowed the winds to stir up the waves and lift them to the skies, while he himself was unmoved by the storm. On the contrary, he walked upon it with marvelous assurance, and, with the waves under his heel, it seemed as though he gloried in braving the untamed element, even during its greatest fury. Similarly, he lets go the reins of our sorrow, unleashing all its force, but in his constancy he accompanies us with steady gait upon the waves, which are constrained to serve as our support. This is the third way in which Jesus Christ overcomes affliction.

We have just seen an image of what transpired in the soul of the Blessed Virgin. When she looked upon the dying Jesus, the waves of sorrow rose up with appalling force, which seemed to threaten heaven itself by attacking her constancy with the most terrible sorrow possible. She plunged to the depths when she saw nothing before her but the horror of death, yet we must not think her to have been troubled by it. Mary did not wish for her troubles to come to an end, because her very troubles made her like her Son. Her affliction knew no limits, because she could not contain her love. She did not want to be consoled, because her Son found no consoler. She did not ask you, O eternal Father, to lessen her sorrow. No, she did not desire to be treated better than her Son. She had to say, with Jesus, "[A]ll thy waves and thy billows have gone over me" (Ps. 42:7). She did not want to lose even a drop of the waters, and she would have been disconsolate not to have faced the same evils as her beloved. Her sorrow could have been raised to infinite heights, but the Holy Spirit would not allow her temple to be destroyed: "the foundations thereof are in the holy mountains" (Ps. 87:1; Douay-Rheims), where the waves could not reach them. Nor could this purest of fountains, which he had preserved with such care from the soil of concupiscence, be troubled by the flood of affliction. This highest part of her soul, in which he had placed his seat, will always keep its serenity, in spite of the tempests that rage beneath it.

To understand the reason, we must meditate further on this mystery. On the eve of his death, the Son of God trembled and shook, so terrible did the expectation of his punishment appear, but in the very grip of his sorrow he seemed to change, and the torment then

At the Cross

seemed as nothing to him. His words to the good thief were measured and calm; he distinctly recognized those who were his own at the foot of the Cross, and he spoke to them and consoled them. Afterward, knowing that in the prophets it was written that a bitter drink was to be prepared for him, he asked for it, tasted it without disgust, and, having said that everything he had to do had been accomplished, gave up his soul to his Father. He accomplished these things so freely, so peacefully, that it is easy to verify what he said: "No one takes [my life] from me, but I lay it down of my own accord" (John 10:18).

The reason we see him so peaceful on Calvary, although he had been so troubled on the Mount of Olives, is that on the Cross and on Calvary he was engaged in the work of his sacrifice. Sacrifice is the action by which we give homage to God. We know from experience that the actions by which we show respect require a composed and controlled countenance. It is the very character of respect. Yet God sees to the very depths of our hearts, and therefore our souls must be composed in order to offer respectful worship. The priest must offer sacrifice with his soul at peace.

O Jesus, my divine Priest, this is why you were so peaceful during your agony. It is true that you were moved on the Mount of Olives, but that was a voluntary anxiety by which you took on the posture and character of a victim. As soon as you were at the altar, and you began to fulfill the function of the priest, as soon as you raised your innocent hands to offer the victim to heaven, you had no more anxiety, nor would you any longer appear fearful, because to have done so would have manifested repugnance for the act. This was so that we would understand that you are a merciful priest who sacrificed yourself willingly, urged on by your love for our salvation.

This is a great mystery, but it was not accomplished in Jesus Christ alone, for he inspired the same sentiments in his holy Mother, who had to take part in this sacrifice. She also had to offer her Son, which is why she was as peaceful as he was, why she stood upright at the foot of the Cross, to manifest a most deliberate action, and, in spite of her sorrow, to offer him with her whole heart to the eternal Father. From her we must learn constantly to sacrifice to God all that is dearest to us. Here is Mary at the foot of the Cross, who rips out her own heart in order to deliver her only Son to death. She offers him, but not only then. She had not ceased to offer him from the day that the good Simeon had predicted the strange contradictions that she would suffer. She had offered him at every moment of her life, and she brought her oblation to its completion at the Cross.

At the Cross

What a horrid sight it was for a mother! O God, he belongs to you. I consent to all of it. Your will be done. Is not my consent required for my Son to be handed over unto death? I am ready to agree to all of it. My deeds will prove my readiness. Unleash all your anger upon him. Do not be content to strike him. Take up your sword to pierce my soul. Tear out my heart. It is Mary who speaks to us, telling us that we must give to God all that is dearest to us. Is that a spouse? Is that a child? You will not lose anything by putting what you most prize into his hands. He will restore it all to you, and a hundredfold besides. Mary received far more than she gave. God soon restored her beloved Son.

18

Behold Thy Mother

It belongs to the Beloved Disciple, the dear son of the Blessed Virgin and the first of the children Jesus gave to her at the Cross, to tell us of the mystery of her marvelous fertility: "A great portent appeared in heaven, a woman clothed with the sun, with the moon under her feet, and on her head a crown of twelve stars; she was with child and she cried out in her pangs of birth, in anguish for delivery" (Rev. 12:1–2). St. Augustine assures us that this woman is the Blessed Virgin, and it is a simple matter to show that she is by several convincing proofs. Yet how are we to understand her birth pangs? We know, because it is the faith of the Church, that Mary was exempt from the common curse upon mothers and that she gave birth without pain just as she had conceived without loss of her virginity. How then are we to reconcile this apparent contradiction?

We must understand that Mary gives birth in two ways. She gave birth to Jesus, and she gives birth to the faithful; that is, she gave birth to the Innocent One, and she gives birth to sinners. She gave birth to the Innocent One painlessly, but she gives birth to sinners with sorrow and anguish. We shall be convinced of this truth if we consider attentively the price she paid to purchase them. What they cost her was her only Son; she could be the mother of Christians only by giving her beloved up to death: O sorrowful fruitfulness! Who can remain unmoved at such a sight?

We cannot sufficiently admire the immense charity by which God chose us to be his children. His Son, equal to himself and begotten from all eternity, is the delight of his heart, and yet, O Goodness, O Mercy, this Father, although having so perfect a Son, did yet adopt others. His charity toward men, his inexhaustible and superabundant love, causes him to give brothers to his firstborn, companions to his only-begotten, and coheirs to the beloved of his heart.

And he does something more, that you will soon see on Calvary. Not only does he join to his own Son the children whom he has adopted by his mercy, but, what surpasses all belief, he gives over his only Son to death in order to give birth to these adoptive ones. Who would wish to adopt a child at such a price? This is, however, just what the eternal Father did.

Jesus teaches us as much in his Gospel. "God so loved the world that he gave his only Son, that whoever believes in him should not perish but have eternal life" (John 3:16). It is the same charity of the Father that gives up the Son, abandons him, and sacrifices him, that adopts us, gives life to us, and regenerates us.

We must not think that Mary paid a lesser price. She is the Eve of the new covenant and the common Mother of all the faithful, and it was ordained that she be joined to the eternal Father and that they give over their common Son to his execution with one accord. It was for this reason that providence called her to the foot of the Cross. She went there to sacrifice her son — to let him die, so that man may live! She went there to receive new children: "Woman," said Jesus, "behold, your son" (John 19:26).

This is a truly anguished birth! What were her sentiments, when she heard the dying voice of her Son? Of all the swords that pierced her soul, surely this was the most sorrowful. "Woman, behold, your son." Surely this, she said, is the last goodbye. My Son, is it with this blow that you leave me? Alas, what son do you give me in place of you? Must John have cost me so dearly? What! A mortal man for a man-God? What a cruel exchange. What a sad and unfortunate consolation.

Behold Thy Mother

O divine Savior, it was not your purpose to console her as much as it was to make her grief immortal. She was accustomed to loving God and now found in his place only a mortal man, and she was well aware of the difference. This son whom you gave to her seems more a reminder of her misery than a consolation for her loss. These words brought her death while they also made her fruitful: she became the mother of Christians while undergoing almost limitless affliction. These new children were drawn forth from her womb by the sword, and her heart was pierced with incredible violence in order to place within it the love of a mother that she would need to have for all the faithful.

Christians, children of Mary, children of her grief, children of blood and of sorrow, can you listen without tears to the evil you have brought upon your Mother? Can you forget the agony with which she gave birth to you? "Forget not the groans of thy mother" (Ecclus. 7:29, Douay-Rheims). Christian, child of the Cross, to you these words are addressed. When the world would beguile you with its luxury, you must avert your imagination from its pernicious delights by remembering the tears of Mary: forget not the groans of this most charitable Mother. Amid violent temptations, when your strength is almost worn down, when your feet stumble in the right path, when bad examples or the ardor of youth press upon you, forget not the groans of your Mother. Remember the tears of Mary. Remember the cruel sorrow with which you shredded her heart on Calvary, and be moved by a mother's cry. What are you thinking, wretch? Do you want to raise up another Cross to nail Jesus to it? Do you want Mary to see her Son crucified again? Do you want to crown her head with thorns, trample underfoot the blood of the New Testament before her very eyes, and reopen all the wounds of her maternal love?

May it please God to prevent us from being so heartless. Let us be moved by a mother's cry. My children, she says, until now I have not suffered at all; I count for naught all the sorrow that afflicted me at the Cross. The blow that you have dealt me by your sins, this is what wounds me. I have watched my beloved Son die, but because he suffered for your salvation, I myself consented to his sacrifice. I drank the bitter cup with joy. My children, believe in my love. To me it seems that this wound is nothing when I compare it to the sorrow that your impenitence gives me. When I see you sacrifice your souls to the fury of Satan; when I see you waste the blood of my Son by making his grace useless, making a plaything of his Cross by your profanation of the sacraments, insulting his mercy by abusing his patience for so long; when I see

Behold Thy Mother

you add insolence to crime, and when among so many sins you have disdain for the remedy of penitence, which you turn into a poison by falling away again and again, amassing a treasure of eternal fury by your hardened and impenitent hearts: it is then that I am cut to the quick. It is then, my children, that my heart is pierced.

19

New Life

Love gives new life to the heart. By its nature, the heart lives for itself; when it is struck by love, it begins a new life for the one it loves. So the Blessed Virgin lived by the strength of her love. Her condition was one of mortal sorrow, a crucifying sorrow, and, amid this sorrow, she lived by love. She always kept before her eyes Jesus Christ crucified. For the efficacy of faith is such that, if St. Paul was able to say to the Galatians that Jesus was crucified before their eyes (Gal. 3:1), how much more was the Blessed Virgin able to remain in the presence of her Son, cruelly torn, bleeding, and dying from his many wounds.

Being always mindful of the Cross and the sufferings of Jesus, she led a life of sorrow and death and was able to say with the apostle, "I die every day" (1 Cor. 15:31). But love came to her aid and supported her in her grief. A vigorous desire to conform herself to the will of her

New Life

beloved made her grief bearable, and Jesus alone lived in her, because she lived only for his love.

The martyrs were animated by a desire to suffer that spurred their courage, upheld their strength, and at the same time prolonged their lives. In order to be conformed to the crucified life of Jesus, Mary always kept Jesus crucified before her eyes; she lived a life of sorrow, and her love made that sorrow bearable because of her desire to be conformed to Jesus, to be pierced by his nails, to be attached to his Cross.

Mary lived only to suffer: "Sustain me with raisins, refresh me with apples; for I am sick with love" (Song of Sol. 2:5). Her love, always languishing because of her sorrow, sought support. What support? The raisins of Calvary and the apples of the Cross. The raisins of Calvary are the thorns; the apples of Calvary are the pain Jesus bore. This is the support that the languishing love of Mary sought. The love of Jesus crucified made her live in this life: in her eyes she saw Jesus crucified, and by her ears she heard the last cry of her beloved as he expired, a terrible cry that rent her heart.

This love also makes us live for souls. By her interior suffering, Mary fulfilled "what is lacking in Christ's afflictions" (Col. 1:24). It seems that he wanted to leave her in the world after him in order to console his Church, his widowed and desolate Spouse. "The voice of the turtle-dove is heard ... turn, my beloved" (Song of Sol. 2:12, 17). This is the cry of the Church, who calls out for the dear spouse she had possessed for a mere moment.

O the cruel one, she cries, O the pitiless one! For how many centuries did we wait for him, and with how much desire! The synagogue did not see him, but the Church saw him, heard him, and touched him, and then, all at once, he left her. O the cruelty! She says to him, with St. Peter, "[W]e have left everything and followed you" (Matt. 19:27). Yet he married her, taking her poverty and detachment for his dowry. And just as soon as he married her, he died, and if he rose from the dead, it was to return whence he came, and he left his chaste Spouse upon the earth, a young and desolate widow.

Mary was given as the unique consolation of all the faithful on earth. She sees her son in all his members. Her compassion is a prayer for all who suffer. Her heart is in the heart of all who weep, to help them to cry for mercy; in the wounds of all the injured, to help them cry for help; in every charitable heart, to press it to lend assistance and consolation to those who need it; in every apostle, to announce the Gospel; in every martyr, that he may be sealed with blood; and, finally, in the hearts of all the faithful, that they may observe what they

New Life

are commanded, profit from counsel, and imitate good examples.

The support for this condition of ours is Holy Communion. "With great delight I sat in his shadow, and his fruit was sweet to my taste" (Song of Sol. 2:3). St. Bernard explained:

> His fruit is his body, and his shadow is faith. Mary sat in the shadow of her own Son, while we sit in the shadow of our faith in the Lord. Why should his fruit not delight us, since we eat it in the holy mysteries? The spouse desires to be covered by the shadow of the one from whom she is to receive refreshment and nourishment. The other trees of the forest may console by their shade, but they do not give any nourishment and they do not produce the fruit of salvation. One alone, the author of life, is able to say to his spouse, I am your salvation. And so she desires to sit in the shadow of Christ, because he alone not only refreshes us by protecting us from the heat of vice, but fills our hearts with the love of virtue.

Since we cannot enjoy the light itself, let us at least rest ourselves in the shade, but let us seek out a tree that can give us not only shade, but also fruit, and not only refreshment, but also nourishment. Only one can do so: Jesus Christ in Holy Communion. Let us then rest our love—languishing and fading for want of possessing the truth—under his shade. He is our only support.

20

God Alone

The love of God brings with it a detachment and solitude that our nature is incapable of bearing and so horrid a destruction of the person and so profound an annihilation of all created things that the senses are overwhelmed. For we must so completely strip ourselves of things in order to attain God that nothing remains to hold us here. The deepest cause of this separation is the jealousy of a God who cannot suffer the presence of another in the heart he wants to love.

It is in the Gospel about St. Martha that we learn how sensitive God is in his jealousy. She is busy and anxious, and all in his service, but he is jealous nevertheless, because she busies herself with what is for him rather than occupying herself completely and solely with him, as Mary did. "Martha, Martha," he said, "you are anxious and troubled about many things; one thing is needful" (Luke 10:41–42). From these words we are able to understand the frightening solitude that this jealous God asks of us. He wants us to cast down, to destroy, to die to all that is not him. As for himself, he hides and gives us almost no access to himself, so that the soul, on one side detached from everything around it, and on the other not finding the means to possess God effectively, falls into weakness, languor, and deep swoons, and, when love reaches its perfection, the swoons become so deep as to carry it to the brink of death and nonbeing. This kind of destruction and death to self is an effect of the Cross.

God reduces everything to so simple a unity that all of nature is appalled. Listen to your heart speak to you. When you hear that we are to love God and him alone, your heart feels itself cast into a fearful solitude in a barren desert, wrenched away from all that it holds dear. To have God and him alone! What then will we do? What will we think about? What of our possessions, our pleasures, our work? This unity seems to us to be a kind of death, because in it we no longer see the delights and charms of the senses, the agreeable distractions among which we seem to enjoy our freedom, nor indeed any of those things without which we think life would be unbearable.

Yet here is what gives the death blow: the heart, stripped of all its superfluous loves, is attracted to the one

God Alone

thing necessary with an incredible force, and, not finding it, kills itself with anxiety. "The unspiritual man does not receive the gifts of the Spirit of God, for they are folly to him, and he is not able to understand them" (1 Cor. 2:14). The soul that has had all sensible objects stripped away now seeks an object that is so simple and inaccessible that it cannot be reached. The soul sees him only through faith, which is to say, she does not see him, and she embraces him only amid darkness and shadows.

What is it that you are doing, O Jesus Christ, the God who was slain? Of what use are your nails, your thorns, and your Cross? Why your death and burial? Was it not to destroy, to crucify, and to bury all things with you? These instruments of your punishment and death are no longer of any use to you, but your Church and the souls you have redeemed ask you for them.

Give to the souls of the baptized, O "bridegroom of blood" (Exod. 4:26), these ravaging and destructive weapons, so that they can be joined to you in the mystery of your Cross. Then their poverty, detachment, and renunciation of self can be the dowry that they bring to you. Purify by the mystery of your Cross the souls you have redeemed, so that they may be made worthy of the mystery of your glory when God will "reconcile to himself all things" (Col. 1:20) in and through you. This is the mystery of unity after which our exiled souls pine, weeping by the waters of Babylon as we remember Zion. This is the mystery of unity that is daily at work through this inexplicable martyrdom, but which will at last be consummated in a peace that is God himself.

These words can give us only an imperfect conception of the love of the Blessed Virgin during the days of her exile and captivity. No, the seraphim themselves can neither understand nor explain Mary's desire for her beloved nor the violence her heart endured while they were separated. If there ever was a soul penetrated by the Cross, it was Mary's. She was always swooning, always dying, always calling upon her beloved in mortal anguish and saying to him: "turn, my beloved, be like a gazelle, or a young stag upon rugged mountains" (Song of Sol. 2:17). It was in vain that her Son had said to her, "yet a little while, and the coming one shall come" (Heb. 10:37), and "a little while, and you will see me no more; again a little while, and you will see me" (John 16:16).

What are you saying, O Jesus? Do you count as a small thing so many years of so horrible a privation? Ah, when one loves you well, a moment is an eternity, for you are eternity itself, and the moments are beyond counting when one knows that at every moment all of eternity is lost. And yet you say "a little while"! This is

God Alone

not to console; this is rather to bring insult to love and its sorrows, to laugh at its impatience and its intolerable excesses.

Savior Jesus, enkindle your love in our hearts by a similar impatience, and because the intimate union that you have with Mary was born in her, fill us with your holy mysteries, dwell in us in the same way by our participation in your Body and Blood, that, living more in you than in ourselves, we will breathe for no other thing than to be consumed with you in the glory that you have prepared for us.

21

A Happy Death

Nature and grace together establish an immutable necessity of dying. It is a law of nature that all mortal things owe their tribute to death, and grace has not exempted mankind from this common necessity. The Son of God, having resolved to defeat death by dying, promulgated this law for us, so that we must pass through the hands of death in order to escape its grasp, we must enter the tomb in order to be reborn, and we must die once in order to strip mortality of its power. And so the death of the Blessed Virgin was a necessary part of her triumph: she had to submit to the law of death in order to leave behind her mortality.

We must not suppose, however, that in submitting to the common law, she did so in an ordinary way. Everything about Mary is supernatural: a miracle gave Jesus Christ to her, and her life, full of miracles, came to an end by a death that was entirely divine. What was the

A Happy Death

principle of this admirable death? It was her love, maternal and divine, that brought it about. It was love that carried off Mary's soul and which, breaking the bonds of her body, the bonds that were keeping her from rejoining her son, at last reunited them in heaven.

Mary's love was made by a flowing forth of the heart of God into her own heart, and the love that she had for her Son came from the same source that gave her that Son. What can human reason say in the face of this mystery? Do we pretend to comprehend the union of Mary and Jesus? We should not even attempt to explain the nature of a maternal love from so exalted a source, which is a participation in the love of the Father for his only-begotten Son. If we cannot understand its force or strength, how shall we imagine the emotions it generated? All we are able to understand is that there never was so great a human emotion as Mary's longing to be reunited to Jesus, nor any violence like the one her heart suffered from their separation.

We need seek no other cause for her death. This love was so ardent that one of its sighs alone would have sufficed to break the bonds of its mortal body. One of its regrets was sufficient to disturb the harmony of her being. A single desire sent heavenward was enough to draw forth Mary's soul. Mary's death was less of a miracle than the continual miracle of her remaining alive while separated from her beloved.

How did this miracle come to an end? How did her love strike the final blow that brought about her death? Was there one single desire that was more ardent, some movement of her soul that was more powerful, or some transport more violent than the others that detached her soul from her body? No, it seems reasonable to attribute her death not to one extraordinary movement, but rather to the very perfection of love. For as this divine love reigned in her heart and occupied all her thoughts, it grew from day to day by its own activity, growing in perfection on the strength of its own desire, increasing by itself until it arrived at such a level of perfection that the earth could no longer contain it.

O love of the Blessed Virgin! Your perfection was too great, you could no longer be held in a mortal body. Your fire gave off flames too hot to be covered by these ashes: go now before the face of God and leap forth within his immensity, which alone can contain it.

And so, the divine Virgin gave up her soul, painlessly and peacefully, putting it in the hands of her Son. It was not necessary that her love break forth by an extraordinary movement. Just as the slightest touch suffices to pull a ripe fruit from the tree, so was this blessed soul gathered

A Happy Death

in, to be immediately transported to heaven. Thus did the divine Virgin die by a movement of divine love. Her soul was carried to heaven upon a cloud of sacred desires, which is what made the angels say: "Who is she that goeth up by the desert, as a pillar of smoke of aromatical spices, of myrrh, and frankincense, and of all the powders of the perfumer?" (Cant. 3:6, Douay-Rheims). This beautiful comparison expresses the manner of her happy and peaceful death. As a mild and gentle heat suffices to free the aromatic vapors from incense, so did a divine warmth separate the Blessed Virgin's soul from her body. There was no overthrowing of the foundations by some violent force; she was gently lifted up to her beloved on a cloud of holy desires. This was her triumphant chariot; her love had built it.

Let us learn from her love to desire Jesus Christ, who is infinitely desirable. And what does Jesus desire? Will he find a heart that pines for him? Such a chaste longing is rarely found in this world, and it is a sure mark of the paltriness of our desire for Jesus if we are content to enjoy the good things of the earth. When fortune smiles upon us, and when we have all the wealth that we require for pleasure and health, do we nonetheless wish for another paradise? Do we imagine that there could be another happiness? If we let our heart speak to us, will it tell us how content it is with this life? If this be our condition, we may be assured that we are not Christians. And if we wish to be Christians, we know what we must do. We must believe that everything is lacking to us, even though the world thinks that we have all that we need. We must groan in prosperity, and we must hope for rest only when we will be with Jesus. Otherwise, the words of St. Augustine will apply to us: "If you do not groan like a pilgrim, you will not rejoice like a citizen." That is to say that you will never be an inhabitant of heaven because you wished to be one of the earth. Refusing the labors of the journey, you will not enjoy the repose of the fatherland, and resting when you should have been marching, you will never arrive at your destination. This is why Mary always wept in remembrance of Zion: her heart could have no peace as long as it was separated from her beloved. At last her desire took her to him, by means of a happy death.

22

Glorified by Purity

Mary's sacred body, the throne of chastity, the temple of Incarnate Wisdom, the instrument of the Holy Spirit, and the seat of the power of the Most High, could not remain in the tomb. The triumph of Mary would have been imperfect if her holy body, which was in a way the source of her glory, had not participated in it. Let us admire this triumph and contemplate the three miracles that holy virginity worked in her. Holy virginity preserved her from corruption, and thus preserved her life. Holy virginity drew down upon her a heavenly influence that caused her to be raised up before the end of time, and thus restored her life. Holy virginity poured out divine light upon her, and thus gave her glory.

Mary's holy virginity was like a divine ointment that preserved her body from corruption. In order to conceive of her purity, we must first consider that Jesus, our Savior, was united so closely to the Blessed Virgin that the union had to be accompanied by a perfect conformity of body and mind. Jesus sought his like, and this is why this spouse of virgins wanted to have a virgin mother, so as to establish that resemblance as the foundation of their union. Yet we must not think that there was anything ordinary about Mary's purity: it gave her perfect integrity of body and soul. This extraordinary grace was poured out upon her like a heavenly dew, and it not only tempered the fires of concupiscence as it does in other Christians, but extinguished them altogether. That is, not only were the flames of the evil deeds, desires, and inclinations of concupiscence extinguished in her, but so was the fire itself, that is, the deepest root and most intimate cause of evil. That being so, how could the flesh of the Blessed Virgin be subject to corruption, since her perfect conformity with Jesus in her virginity of body and mind had removed the very principle of bodily corruption?

We must not think of the corruption of the body as the art of medicine does, as though it were merely the natural consequence of the mixture of elements in our bodies. We must lift our minds higher and understand that the flesh is subject to the necessity of corruption because it is a harbor of evil, a source of wrongful desires, and a "sinful flesh," as St. Paul calls it (Rom. 8:3). Such a flesh ought to be destroyed, even in the case of

Glorified by Purity

the elect, because in its sinfulness it does not merit to be reunited with the souls of the blessed nor to enter into the kingdom of heaven: "flesh and blood cannot inherit the kingdom of God" (1 Cor. 15:50). It must, therefore, exchange its form so that it may be renewed and lose all of its first being in order to receive a second one from the hand of God. Like an old ramshackle building that is allowed to fall down bit by bit so that a new one can be built in a more beautiful architectural style, so also with this flesh made disorderly by concupiscence. God allows it to fall into ruin, so that he can rebuild it in accord with the initial plan of Creation. This is how we ought to think about the corruption of the flesh, according to the principles of the gospel, and, accordingly, we ought to understand that Mary, being entirely pure, was consequently incorruptible.

It is for the same reason that she was granted immortality by an early resurrection. For although God has marked out the time of the general resurrection of the dead, there are reasons that justify anticipating that time in favor of the Blessed Virgin. The sun ripens each fruit in its season, yet there are orchards so well tended that their fruit ripens early. There are also trees in the Spouse's garden that bear their fruit sooner. Mary's conformity with Jesus disposes her to receive a more prompt effect of his life-giving power. She is certainly able to attract his power, just as she attracted his very self. He became incarnate in this flesh, being charmed by her purity, and he loved this flesh so much that he remained within it for nine months. He will not allow it to remain in the tomb, but he will transport it into heaven, where it is arrayed with immortal glory.

It is holy virginity that gives Mary this glorious raiment. In his Gospel, Jesus tells us about the glory of resurrected bodies with this lovely phrase: "in the resurrection ... they are like angels in heaven" (Matt. 22:30). Now, of all the Christian virtues, the one that is best able to produce such an effect is chastity, for that is what makes there be angels on earth and in the world to come. There is good reason to be assured that purity has a special power to contribute to the glory of the resurrected body. Let us consider then what brilliance and light will surround Mary, whose purity surpasses even that of the seraphim. Holy Scripture seeks out extraordinary expressions to represent such great brilliance. There is not enough light in the world to trace even an image of it; all of nature's luminous bodies must be gathered together to do so. She has the moon at her feet and a crown of stars around her head; the sun penetrates her and surrounds her with its rays. She is "a woman clothed with the sun"

Glorified by Purity

(Rev. 12:1), so much glory and brilliance is required to adorn this purest of women.

Let us then learn to esteem the sacred treasure that we carry in our earthen vessels (2 Cor. 4:7). Let us daily renew our love for purity and keep it unstained by the least attachment to our bodies. And if we are jealous of the purity of our flesh, all the more should we be of the purity of our minds. By this means, we may be worthy companions of blessed Mary, and, holding her glorious train, we will walk closely behind her as she climbs to her throne.

23

Crowned with Humility

Humility brought about the triumph of Jesus and so must also be the cause of Mary's glory. She was exalted because of her humility, and in the following manner. We recall that it belongs to the humble person to impoverish himself and strip himself of his advantages. Yet, by a marvelous exchange, humility enriches by stripping away, because it restores all that it takes away. Nothing is more fitting to humility than these words of St. Paul: "as having nothing, and yet possessing everything" (2 Cor. 6:10).

The Blessed Virgin possessed three precious goods: high rank, an admirable purity of body and mind, and, what is above every treasure, Jesus Christ himself. She had a beloved Son, in whom "all the fulness of God was pleased to dwell" (Col. 1:19). Here is a creature different from every other creature, but her very great humility stripped her, in a certain sense, of these advantages.

Crowned with Humility

Elevated above all others by her dignity as the Mother of God, she placed herself among the common people by living as a servant. Separated from all of us by her immaculate purity, she shared the condition of sinners by purifying herself with the rest. Thus we see her prerogatives stripped away by her humility. But there is something more: she even lost her Son on Calvary, and not only because he died, but also because in a certain sense he ceased to be her Son when he substituted another for himself, saying to her, "Woman, behold, your son."

Let us meditate on this. It seems as though the Savior no longer knew his mother, for he called her Woman rather than Mother. There is a mystery here: he is in a condition of humiliation, and it is necessary for his Mother to share in it with him. Jesus has God for his Father, and Mary has God for her Son. But the Divine Savior lost his Father and now speaks of him only as his God. Thus, Mary will lose her Son, who now calls her only by the name Woman. And more humiliation is in store: in giving Mary John for her son, Jesus is acting as though henceforth he will cease to be her Son, as if the sacred bond has been broken. This is why he said it: during the years of his mortal life, he fulfilled the duties of a son toward Mary and was her consolation and only support in her old age. Now that he is about to enter into his glory, he takes on sentiments more worthy of God and leaves to another the duties of natural piety.

Mary no longer has her Son, and she will live through a long series of years in this condition. John for Jesus, the servant for the master, the son of Zebedee for the Son of God. It pleased the Son thus to humiliate her. St. John takes the liberty of recognizing her as his Mother, and she humbly accepts the exchange. How deep is her humility! How wonderful her obedience!

Let us gather together into one all of these acts of humility of the Blessed Virgin. Her high rank is covered with the mantle of servitude. Her purity is hidden under the marks of sin. She even loses her Son and consents to have another in his place. Her humility has stripped everything away. Yet we also see that this humility restores every advantage to her: "as having nothing, yet as possessing everything."

O Mother of Jesus, because you called yourself a servant, today humility prepares a throne for you: climb up to this high place and receive absolute rule over every creature. O Virgin, all holy and all pure, more pure than the rays of the sun, you chose to purify yourself and to be counted among sinners, and your humility will raise you up; you will be the advocate for all sinners, and you will be their principal refuge and hope after Jesus Christ. You

Crowned with Humility

lost your Son, and it seemed that he had abandoned you to a foreign land, but because you submitted to such a humiliation with patience, your Son reclaims his rights, he holds out his hand to you, and the whole celestial court admires you, O Happy Virgin, as you rise into heaven: "Who is that coming up from the wilderness, leaning upon her beloved?" (Song of Sol. 8:5). This is the royal entry of the Blessed Virgin. The sacred ceremony is finished. Mary is placed upon her throne, in the arms of her Son, in the eternal noontime of heaven, and it is holy humility that has accomplished the work.

It is now for us to pay our respects to this great Queen and, seeing her so close to her Son, to pray her to assist us by her all-powerful intercession. O holy, blessed Mary, because you are with Jesus, enjoying a holy and blessed familiarity with him, speak for us to his heart. Speak, and your Son will listen. We do not ask you for human glory. Obtain for us only that humility by which you have been crowned. May all those who celebrate your triumph enter profoundly into the knowledge that there is no glory except that which is founded upon humility and nothing truer than the words of the Gospel: the one who humbles himself in this life shall be exalted forever in the eternal joy to which we are being led by the Father, Son, and Holy Spirit. Amen.

24

Jesus through Mary

Having resolved from all eternity to give us Jesus through Mary, God was not content to make use of her as an instrument. Rather, he wished her to cooperate in this great work by a movement of her will. This is why he sent his angel to her to propose the mystery. The great work of the Incarnation, which held heaven and earth in suspense for so many centuries, could not be achieved until Mary's consent had been given. It was necessary for mankind that she desire our salvation. She did will it, and it pleased the eternal Father that Mary should contribute to the work of giving the world its Savior.

This truth is well known, but there is a consequence of it that is not sufficiently pondered. Divine Wisdom having once resolved to give us Jesus through the Blessed Virgin, the decree is now unchanging. Her maternal charity having contributed so much to our salvation in the mystery of the Incarnation, the universal source of

Jesus through Mary

grace, it will now contribute eternally in all its other operations, which are so many dependent parts of it. To understand this, we must note the three chief operations of the grace of Christ. God calls us, justifies us, and enables us to persevere. Vocation is the first step; justification is the progress we make; perseverance is the journey's end. In these three stages, the work of Christ is required. Yet we see in the Scriptures that the charity of the Blessed Virgin is joined to them as well.

With respect to vocation, consider what happened to St. John the Baptist while he was in his mother's womb, and you will see an image of sinners called by grace. John is in darkness: he can neither see nor hear. Jesus comes to him without his knowing it. Jesus approaches; he speaks to his heart; he awakens and draws to himself this sleeping and insensible heart. This is how the Son of God treats the sinners whom he calls, but he shows us in St. John's case that the Virgin's charity worked together with him. What made Jesus come to John if not the charity of the Blessed Virgin? If Jesus acted in John's heart, was it not at the sound of his Mother's voice? In the case of St. John the Baptist, then, we see Mary as the Mother of those whom Jesus calls.

Let us now consider those whom he justifies: the disciples of the Son of God, at the wedding at Cana in

Meditations on Mary

Galilee. They had already been called, but they are not yet justified because they do not believe in their Master. Listen to the Evangelist: "This, the first of his signs, Jesus did at Cana in Galilee, and manifested his glory; and his disciples believed in him" (John 2:11). Could he have expressed himself in clearer terms about their justification by faith as a consequence of this miracle? Nor could he have better explained the part played by the Blessed Virgin. For who does not know that this great miracle was the effect of her charity and prayers? Was it in vain that the Son of God—who disposes all things so well—wished to perform his first miracle at his mother's request? Who does not admire her role in this miracle, which was immediately followed by the justification of the apostles? Was this an accident? Does it not rather seem that the Holy Spirit wants us to understand, as St. Augustine noted in his interpretation of this event, that blessed Mary, "being the mother of our head according to the flesh, had to be the mother of his members according to the spirit and cooperate by her charity in their spiritual birth"?

It is not enough that she contributed to their birth; let us also consider how Mary effects the holy perseverance of the children of God. Come then, children of adoption and eternal predestination, children of mercy and

Jesus through Mary

grace, faithful companions of the Savior, who persevere with him to the end, run to the Blessed Virgin and range yourselves with the others under the wings of her maternal charity. Christians, here is the Beloved Disciple of our Savior to represent us at Calvary: he is the figure of those who persevere, for he followed Jesus even to the Cross and attached himself so firmly to the mystical wood that he was ready to die with him. He is therefore the figure of those who persevere, and we see Jesus give him to his Mother: "Woman, behold, your son." Those who understand how full of mysteries are the Scriptures will understand from these three examples that the charity of Mary is a general instrument of the operations of grace.

Let us rejoice in our protector. The night with its terrors has passed; the day approaches, hope comes, and we see a first ray of it shining in the protection of the Blessed Virgin. She was born to bring us aid; it would not be possible to choose a better advocate. Let us pray that she will speak for us to the heart of her Son. Yes, certainly, O Mary, it belongs to you to speak to the heart; you have a faithful correspondent there, that is, filial love, which advances to receive maternal love and which anticipates your desires. Should you fear to be refused when you speak to the Savior? His love intercedes in your favor, for nature itself solicits on your behalf. We readily grant

Meditations on Mary

requests when we are already conquered by affection. It is for this reason that Mary always speaks efficaciously, because she speaks to the heart of a Son. Let her then speak boldly on our behalf to the heart of Jesus.

What grace shall she ask for us? What do we desire from her intercession? Do you hesitate? Does not her charity inspire you to desire to be strengthened in charity? It is this that we ask. Without the desire to be charitable, what good does it do for us to call upon the name of Mary? Go on your way with these thoughts in mind: it is Mary who tells you. Do not let the day end without leaving behind some mark of her charity.

Sophia Institute

Sophia Institute is a nonprofit institution that seeks to nurture the spiritual, moral, and cultural life of souls and to spread the Gospel of Christ in conformity with the authentic teachings of the Roman Catholic Church.

Sophia Institute Press fulfills this mission by offering translations, reprints, and new publications that afford readers a rich source of the enduring wisdom of mankind.

Sophia Institute also operates two popular online Catholic resources: CrisisMagazine.com and CatholicExchange.com.

Crisis Magazine provides insightful cultural analysis that arms readers with the arguments necessary for navigating the ideological and theological minefields of the day. *Catholic Exchange* provides world news from a Catholic perspective as well as daily devotionals and articles that will help you to grow in holiness and live a life consistent with the teachings of the Church.

In 2013, Sophia Institute launched Sophia Institute for Teachers to renew and rebuild Catholic culture through service to Catholic education. With the goal of nurturing the spiritual, moral, and cultural life of souls, and an abiding respect for the role and work of teachers, we strive to provide materials and programs that are at once enlightening to the mind and ennobling to the heart; faithful and complete, as well as useful and practical.

Sophia Institute gratefully recognizes the Solidarity Association for preserving and encouraging the growth of our apostolate over the course of many years. Without their generous and timely support, this book would not be in your hands.

www.SophiaInstitute.com
www.CatholicExchange.com
www.CrisisMagazine.com
www.SophiaInstituteforTeachers.org

Sophia Institute Press® is a registered trademark of Sophia Institute.
Sophia Institute is a tax-exempt institution as defined by the
Internal Revenue Code, Section 501(c)(3). Tax I.D. 22-2548708.